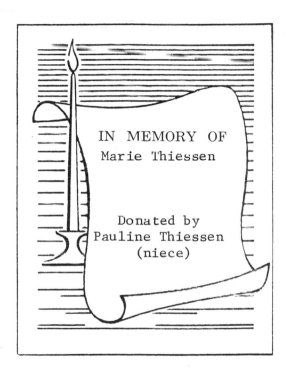

IN MEMORY OF
Marie Thiessen

Donated by
Pauline Thiessen
(niece)

GOSPEL POWER

GOSPEL POWER

TOWARD THE REVITALIZATION OF PREACHING

John Burke, O.P.

ALBA · HOUSE   NEW · YORK

CIETY OF ST. PAUL, 2187 VICTORY BLVD., STATEN ISLAND, NEW YORK 10314

Library of Congress Cataloging in Publication Data

Burke, John, 1928-
    Gospel power : toward the revitalization of preaching.

    1. Preaching. I. Title.
BV4211.2.B85   251   77-14517
ISBN 0-8189-0359-7

Nihil Obstat:
James Luke Prest, O.P., S.T.D.
Censor Deputatus

Imprimatur:
William Cardinal Baum
Archbishop of Washington
August 22, 1977

The Nihil Obstat and Imprimatur
are a declaration that a book or pamphlet is considered
to be free from doctrinal or moral error. It is not implied
that those who have granted the Nihil Obstat and
Imprimatur agree with the contents,
opinions or statements expressed.

Produced in the United States of
America by the Fathers and Brothers of the
Society of St. Paul, 2187 Victory Boulevard,
Staten Island, New York, 10314, as part of their
communications apostolate.

2 3 4 5 6 7 8 9 (Current Printing: first digit).

DEDICATION

To all those men and women who share the Good News of their salvation with others.

CONTENTS

INTRODUCTION

There is a marvelous power in the preaching of the Good News of Jesus Christ: Gospel Power. It changes hearts. renews lives and transforms society. Gospel Power has done it before: Gospel Power will do it again when the Church devotes its massive spiritual and physical energies to the difficult task of revitalizing biblical preaching. While the causes of the severe and debilitating "crisis of faith" are many and complex, one of the significant reasons for the lack of faith in today's world is the poor quality of preaching in the Roman Catholic Church. As Pope Paul VI said in an address in September, 1975:

> If the faith is failing to find hearers and believers, is this because it is taught and preached in an old, abstruse way, cut off from life and contrary to the tendencies and tastes of today? Ought we not renew the kerygma—the announcement of the Christian message—if we want to find hearers and followers?

Clearly there is an urgent need today to find hearers and followers. In the United States, for example, there are 49 million Catholics. almost a quarter of the total population. Of that huge number, 250.000 are "professional" Catholics—bishops, priests, permanent deacons, religious brothers and sisters. in addition to countless numbers of dedicated lay Catholics who are paid to work for the Church. Together with all the faithful they constitute a vast spiritual army in whose ears the last words of Jesus Christ ring with strength and urgency: "Go into the whole world: proclaim the Good News to all creation." Yet. the tragic fact is that in 1976 only 80.000 adults became new members of the Church. in a country in which at least 80 million (and possibly even 101 million) do not belong to any church. Christian or otherwise!

Nor is the problem of finding hearers and followers of Christ limited to the unchurched. In addressing the Bishops' Synod on Evangelization in 1974. Cardinal Krol of Philadelphia remarked:

> [Within the Church] there are also troubling signs. Many Catholics do not regularly attend Mass and receive the sacraments. Vocations to the priesthood and religious life have declined. There is much polarization and controversy—and paradoxically, much religious apathy. Many young people are apparently "turned off" by organized religion. The philosophy of secularism has made deep inroads in Catholic life.

Elsewhere the bishops note with sadness that the voice of secularism in the United States has greater force in the formation of life-style and values than does the voice of Christ's Church.

The task of renewal which the Pope sets for the Church is not limited to bishops and priests because the proclamation of the Christian message is the work of the whole Church and all the elements of its life.

> The duty to proclaim the Gospel belongs to the whole people of God. gathered by the Holy Spirit in the Church through the Word of God and the Eucharist.
>   (Bishops' Synod on Evangelization)

Nevertheless. while recognizing the complexity of the crisis and the need for a total response to it by all members of the Church. it remains true that the burden of the preaching ministry has been given directly to bishops and priests as their primary responsibility. The Second Vatican Council said:

> Among the principal duties of bishops the preaching of the Gospel occupies an eminent place. For bishops are preachers of the faith who lead new disciples to Christ.
> **(Dogmatic Constitution on the Church, No. 25)**

In the **Directory on the Pastoral Ministry of Bishops** issued by the Sacred Congregation of Bishops, this injunction is given to the bishop: "He makes his priests realize that preaching the Word of God is the special and absolutely necessary duty of the pastor of souls." The latter carries out the teaching of the Second Vatican Council which decreed:

> The People of God find unity first of all through the Word of the living God, which is quite properly sought from the lips of priests. Since no one can be saved who has not first believed, priests, as co-workers with their bishops, have as their primary duty the proclamation of the Gospel of God to all.
> **(Decree on the Ministry and Life of Priests, No. 4)**

It is with this understanding of the grave responsibility given to bishops and priests especially to preach the Gospel that this book explores how the preaching ministry can be renewed so that the People of God can truly find life through the hearing of the Word of God in faith.

While the problem of preaching to those who already live within the Church is difficult enough, touching the hearts and minds of those who do not yet believe is even more difficult since in many cases there is no common religious language through which the spiritual search

can be conducted and the satisfaction of the human heart
can be probed. Most traditional theological expressions
no longer reflect vital spiritual realities which form the
pattern of modern living. Many preachers still seem
bound to ecclesiastical traditions and attitudes which are
foreign to contemporary experiences of authority, gov-
ernment, economics and family life. They have become
separated from and out of touch with just plain folks.
There is, consequently, a great need for preachers today
to break with linguistic and liturgical habits of the past
and to explore new avenues of approach to a world which
is no longer impressed by remnant feudal customs of respect, dress or structure.

Unfortunately, the necessary task of out-reach is not
made easier by the seminary training of the clergy, (imitated to a great extent in the formation of permanent
deacons), since by and large it aims at preparing them
to be pastors of souls and defenders of the institutional
Church rather than fishers of men, even though the Chief
Pastor himself wears the Ring of the Fisherman.

In these days of rampant paganism when "the mass
of men lead lives of quiet desparation," Pope Paul VI
wrote his **Apostolic Exhortation on Evangelization in the
Modern World** because he recognized that a new spirit-
uality is needed to shape the hearts and minds of preachers. What is required is that they be filled with the desire
to cast out the net of divine love and draw all men in
through the words they speak in explicit witness to the
saving power of Jesus Christ. The Gospel is an attractive
message of hope and promise which requires that its
preachers themselves be attractive. delightful and inspired. Because nothing is more persuasive than a joy-
filled person, preachers should be filled with happiness
themselves as they proclaim the source of their happiness, Jesus Christ.

At the same time, the richness of the Word of God

and the diversity of the gifts He has given to His people means that there can be no single model for fruitful preaching. The wide-range of personalities called to preach in the Sacred Scriptures is proof enough of that: Moses, Aaron, Jeremiah, Jonah, Amos, Peter, Paul and John. Yet, there is always a temptation to approach effective preaching by examining successful preachers and putting them up as models to be somehow imitated—in our day, men like Archbishop Sheen or Billy Graham. Such an approach can lead to more of a concern for techniques than for the communication of the Gospel message itself and can result in diffidence in or even fear of preaching. If every preacher had to sound like the "great" preachers, Christianity would be poor indeed.

The Gospel message itself, as experienced by the believer gives shape to its proclamation. Preaching is necessarily witness, and witness can never be circumscribed by rules of rhetoric. On the contrary, the more creative the preacher's penetration into the meaning of the Revealed Truth, the more effective his preaching will be and the more unique his expression. Preachers are truly incomparable, since there are as many styles of preaching as there are preachers who do it. The Gospel is one, but how it is experienced in the heart is immensely varied; since it is out of the abundance of the heart that the mouth speaks, the Church can rejoice that diversity and not similarity will mark effective proclamation of the Good News.

The pages that follow are a modest attempt to take a fresh look at what is at the heart of preaching and what is unique to the three different kinds of preaching: evangelization, catechesis and didascalia.

Since the life of faith has different stages of development, over-lapping but different, not all preaching bears fruit equally in all stages of faith development. Evangelization appeals to the unbeliever and brings him to faith in Jesus Christ as Lord and Saviour. Catechesis inspires the believer to live his life in Christ filled with praise and thanksgiving. Didascalia nourishes the mature believer by bringing him to new awareness of the depths of the wisdom and knowledge of God.

The liturgical homily necessarily touches all levels of believers and unbelievers and is, therefore, treated separately.

There is a special problem which listeners encounter in preaching today: the substitution of good advice for the Good News—a concern for human rectitude in place of divine love. It is a tenacious, somewhat complicated, but above all, pervasive problem affecting all three kinds of preaching. It is so grave that an appendix has been added to offer perspectives for correcting it.

The entire theoretical understanding of preaching and the diverse kinds of preaching has no value apart from helping preachers to prepare and to present powerful sermons. The final item, therefore, is a Sermon Evaluation Form which is intended to assist the transfer of the ideas discussed from the printed page to the spoken word—the Word of God.

GOSPEL POWER

CHAPTER ONE

TOWARDS A DEFINITION OF "PREACHING"

The Meaning of Preaching

The term "preaching" has fallen upon hard times. While St. Paul gloried in the fact that he had been sent to preach, today "preacher" implies a man with great enthusiasm but little intellectual perspicacity. As a result, in the Catholic Church almost no preacher lives by the fruit of his preaching alone; it is usually something done on the side in addition to his regular job. Even among parish priests, occasional surveys rank preaching as task number seven or eight out of a possible ten.

"Don't preach to me" reflects how preaching is frequently seen as an offensive intrusion into a person's private affairs—a moralistic put-down of his behavior patterns and value systems. Indeed, preaching is more noted for giving warnings and condemnations than for being the vehicle by which the Infinitely Great and Loving Divine Mind reveals its innermost thoughts, ideas and desires to His beloved sons and daughters whom He has created in his own image and likeness. In short, the proper moral response to the Gospel message has largely replaced the Message itself as the substance of contemporary sermons.

Since preaching as a ministry of the Church has not merited much profound theological reflection in recent times, even a stable vocabulary for preaching is lacking. For example, in the **Constitution on the Sacred Liturgy,** the Council Fathers use a variety of terms interchangeably and without seeming distinction to refer to preaching: "homily **(homilia),**" "admonition **(brevis admonitio),**" "instruction **(institutio, instructio),**" "sermon **(sermo, concio).**" This loose usage of terms is in marked contrast to the ordinary uses of language, but especially theological language, in which specific terms stand for specific realities. **Writing, counseling, teaching, lecturing, or discussing** are clearly distinguished from one another and cause no confustion to the listener or reader.

On the other hand, **preaching** can mean anything. For some, everything a priest does is a form of preaching, whether it be teaching mathematics in a classroom, counseling the distraught in a rectory parlor, visiting the sick in the hospital, or even adding up the parish finances. One priest summed up the present broad connotation of the term when he remarked: "My life is my sermon." Such a sermon can, of course, be inspiring if the preacher is a saint. The reality is that few are saints with the result that few, simply by living out their daily lives, are able to change the lives of others and bring them into union with Jesus Christ as Saviour and Lord. Sincerity and good will are no substitution for the Word of God and the Truth that frees.

The Good News of Salvation needs to be spelled out in words that excite the imagination, inform the mind and enflame the heart. All are called to be saints, only a few to be preachers. The thing that sets the preacher apart is that he talks. He utters words that explain, instruct, inspire, admonish, warn and delight. In short, he speaks the Word of God, and his living utterance of that word by the power of the Holy Spirit who inspires it, gives birth to and nourishes faith in Jesus Christ. The preacher's own faith compels speech which, in its turn, gives birth to faith in the listener. Faith speaks to faith.

Far then, from being the total life of holy people

encompassing all the varied activities of the Church, preaching refers to a very limited, yet essential act of ministry. Technically, preaching can be defined as: A public act of an authorized minister of the Word, in the name of the Church, orally communicating a personally experienced theological insight into the meaning of divine revelation in such a simple, direct, yet sufficiently developed way, that those who listen may share that insight, in faith, in accordance with their measure of the grace of God.

Although succinct, the definition is packed with meaning for today's preacher. An examination of its elements casts light on ways to grow in this vital ministry.

A Public Act

Preaching is described as a public act because of its nature as a divine communication of God to man; it is always addressed to everyone. That is to say, it is not the private conversation of one individual with another, as a counseling session; nor is it the paid-for communication of a teacher to those enrolled in his course. It is not a discussion among equals; rather, it is God proclaiming His love for all to all. And the only requisite for hearing His truth is good will and an open mind.

This does not imply that preaching does not respect the differences that exist among men; there are different kinds of preaching to achieve different purposes and which occur in different situations. For example, the eucharistic homily is proclaimed in the context of the liturgy and is directed towards believing Christians who have gathered together to give thanks and praise to God. Nevertheless, it is the very nature of the word of God to be for all, to attract all and to meet the needs of all. Consequently, no matter what the occasion, all preaching— to be an authentic expression of the Divine Mind—needs to have a certain open-ended quality in which all who listen might find nourishment and strength. Such a quality becomes more apparent when it is considered in contradistinction to that kind of private counseling in which everything that is said is directed solely and totally to meet the individual needs of the person being counseled.

To say, however, that preaching is always a public act is not to imply that it is not also intensely personal. Indeed, because it is universal in its appeal, it is likewise most apt to touch the innermost core of being of each individual person, Scripture itself testifies:

> The word of God is something alive and active; it cuts
> like any double-edged sword but more finely;
> it can slip through the place where the soul is divided
> from the spirit, as joints from the marrow; it can
> judge the secret emotions and thoughts. (Heb 4:12)

Thus "public" in the definition, is not opposed to personal, but to private and self-limiting.

Authorized Minister of the Word

This public act can only be executed by an authorized minister because the preacher speaks not for himself, or of himself; he speaks for God. As St. Paul says: "They will never have a preacher unless one is sent." (Rm 10:15) The preacher proclaims not his own word, but the Word of God; it is the Word of God that gives birth to faith in Jesus Christ. (1 Pet 1:23) No one can speak the Word of God except him who has been sent by God as Jesus was, for "No one knows the Father except the Son and those to whom the Son chooses to reveal Him." (Mt 11:27) To put it another way, the preacher has nothing to say except what God has given him to say; he passes on like St. Paul, what he has first received—the one Gospel of Jesus Christ.

In a more legalistic era of the Church, theological discussion tended to center on the concept of mission: what it is, who could be sent and, above all, how the sending was accomplished. Today there is a new awareness, especially since Pope Paul VI's **Apostolic Exhortation on Evangelization in the Modern World,** that by reason of baptism and confirmation all Christians have some power over the word of God; all are truly sent to be witnesses to Jesus Christ; all are called to proclaim his Lordship. Such proclamation is "a basic duty of the [whole] people of God." **(Ad Gentes,** 35)

Nevertheless, in the Roman Catholic tradition, formal mission equivalent to the special kind of mission given by Jesus to his apostles is given by the Church in two ways: either by ordination or by delegation. When a bishop is consecrated or a priest is ordained, the very sacramental act itself imposes a duty of proclaiming the Word of God. At the same time, the sacred imposition of hands bestows on the recipient the power to proclaim. As a consequence, the duty of proclaiming the Word of God, being a sacramental duty, cannot be impeded except for a just cause. In other words, the priest's duty to preach does not come from the fact that the bishop gives him permission to preach, but rather from the imposition of hands. In the very act of ordination, his bishop—like the elders of the New Testament—sends him forth to preach the Word of God.

On the other hand, if the priest is not faithful to his mission, it is the responsibility of the legitimate Church authority to suspend him from his office of proclamation because he no longer speaks for the Church. However, as long as he is in union with his bishop, from the very fact that he has been ordained he has the responsibility and the privilege of preaching.

The People of God finds its unity first of all through

the Word of the living God, which is quite properly sought from the lips of priests. Since no one can be saved who has not first believed, priests, as co-workers with their bishops, have as their primary duty the proclamation of the gospel of God to all. **(Decree on the Ministry and Life of Priests, No. 4)**

While theirs is the primary responsibility, the ordained clergy alone cannot possibly do all the preaching that is required to build up the Church anew in each generation. Consequently, they have always delegated others who are not ordained also to speak in the name of the Church. Delegation occurs most commonly when lay people are employed as catechists in religious education programs, when lay preachers are used at Mass, or where religious women are deputed to preside at Bible services. **(Constitution on the Sacred Liturgy, No. 35:4)** The laity in such cases have power over the Word of God, not by reason of ordination, but because an ordained minister shares with them his own office of preaching.

It is appropriate to take particular note here of another sacramental source of the power to preach: the sacrament of matrimony. For most Roman Catholics who are "born into the faith," their parents are the first preachers of the Word they ever hear. And it is not to extend the notion of preaching being developed here, to say that sacramental powers and offices bestowed on the married couple include the power as well as the responsibility to bring the Good News of salvation to their own children. Parents may not think of themselves in the front-line of evangelization, but they certainly are. No one else has a greater opportunity to generate a love of Jesus Christ in the hearts of their children than parents; and for the most part, children are the Christians that their parents have formed them to be.

No agency in the Church can ever equal the primal

force of the parents' daily preaching of God's holy word to their children. When the great apostle St. Paul wrote to his faithful disciple Timothy, urging him and advising him to preach the Good News without ceasing, he appealed to Timothy's own training as a child, and asked him to recall to mind the teaching he had received from the mouths of Eunice and Lois, his mother and grandmother. (2 Tm 3:14)

Such power to generate faith does not come simply from the example of the parents' lives; it also requires that they give expression to the revelation of God to which they have assented and by which they live their lives. Preaching, therefore, is not limited to formal Church situations, but it can occur everywhere, and in no place does the act more fittingly occur than in the sacred precincts of the Christian home.

The family is, so to speak, the domestic Church. In it parents should, by their word and example, be the first preachers of the faith to their children. **(Dogmatic Constitution on the Church, No. 11)**

St. Thomas Aquinas describes it with his usual succinct insight as "the conversation of the Christian life."

There is another kind of mission which, although probably not sufficient for ministry in the Roman Catholic tradition, forms the basis for much Protestant preaching: the interior call. That sense of being called by God to proclaim His word is something which occurs frequently in Sacred Scripture as in the experience of St. Paul or the prophets of the Old Testament. Jeremiah, in fact, complained because he found his call to preach irresistable:

You have seduced me, Yahweh,
and I have let myself be seduced;
you have overpowered me: you were stronger.

I am a daily laughing-stock,
everybody's butt.
Each time I speak the word, I have to howl
and proclaim: 'Violence and ruin!'
The word of Yahweh has meant for me
insult, derision, all day long.
I used to say, "I will not think about him,
I will not speak in his name any more.'
imprisoned in my bones.
The effort to restrain it wearied me,
I could not bear it. (Jr 20:7-9)

In the Roman Catholic tradition, for this call to be legitimized in the public ministry of the Church, its ratification by Church leaders is required either sacramentally or by delegation. In spite of this, it nevertheless seems to be essential for truly effective preaching that the one who preaches be filled with a strong sense of being sent by God Himself to proclaim His word.

In The Name of the Church

Authorization, whether by ordination or delegation, is necessary because the preacher can proclaim only what the Christian community believes and celebrates. He does not speak as a private individual; he is a spokesman—mouthpiece—for God and God's Church. The preacher's teaching does not originate with himself; he has received it from those who walked with Jesus and were especially appointed by Him to be His witnesses. The Church of Christ formed by the apostles forms the modern preacher in the Gospel, and it is this Gospel, of which he is only a minister, that gives birth to faith in the Risen Jesus.

St. Paul stresses the necessity of fidelity to the Gospel when he writes:

> Let me warn you that if anyone preaches a version
> of the Good News different from the one we have
> already preached to you, whether it be ourselves or
> an angel from heaven, he is to be condemned. (Gal 1:8)

Further on, he gives the reason for the unchangeable
character of the Gospel:

> The Good News I preached is not a human
> message that I was given by men; it is something I
> learned only through a revelation of Jesus
> Christ. (Gal 1:11)

Stressing the importance of fidelity to the Gospel and
the communal nature of the faith that is preached raises
rather serious theological problems when it comes to
preachers' drawing out "gospel conclusions" relative to
controversial social and political issues. While in no way
supporting the view that current problems should not be
addressed by preachers, there remains some justification
for the restlessness of the Christian faithful when subjected to preaching in which practical applications are
not in harmonious balance with scriptural and doctrinal
content. Faith in Jesus is engendered by fidelity to the
Gospel, and not by well-intentioned yet disputable responses to it. Frequently, indeed, the response that is
"demanded" by the Gospel is preached in place of the
Gospel itself which is assumed to be believed and, therefore, it is neglected. Faith in the Message, however,
must precede any exhortation to carry out that faith in
terms of a lived response, and not every believer will
see the response in exactly the same way. Consequently, every preacher would do well to take as much care
as the great apostle, Paul, in sorting out "what is from
the Lord" and "what is from me." (1 Cor 7:10-12, 25)

The problem becomes particularly acute when Church

leaders express themselves on contemporary issues in a manner which seems to demand a faith assent, when in fact the arguments leading to the demand are not clear, cogent or necessary. To be specific, is it "gospel" that the United States have an anti-abortion amendment to the Constitution, or is there some freedom with regard to the selection of the means of achieving gospel values?

While the raising of this question is discomforting, it is necessary, especially in a democracy. Belief in Jesus is not the result of legislative force but evangelical acceptance, and the preaching of the Good News and the moral response to it must be in conformity to the freedom with which God has blessed His beloved children.

The Decree on the Ministry and Life of Priests, No. 6, gives an excellent perspective for solving the difficulty by its recognition that all believers are guided in their Christian lives by the Holy Spirit and the love of Christ.

As educators in the faith, priests must see to it, either by themselves or through others, that the faithful are led individually in the Holy Spirit to a development of their own vocation as required by the gospel, to a sincere and active charity, and to that freedom with which Christ has made us free.

In building the Christian community, priests are never to put themselves at the service of any ideology or human faction. Rather, as heralds of the gospel and shepherds of the Church, they must devote themselves to the spiritual growth of the Body of Christ.

Oral Communication

Unlike a book or an article in a theological journal that can be catalogued and enshrined forever, a sermon is a fleeting reality which exists only in the single moment of utterance. Its being does not last beyond the sound of the voice, yet God has chosen that fragile vehicle to change lives. The sermon is not the outline or the manuscript; it is the preacher, totally involved in speaking what he believes and has experienced to be true, who is the means of salvation. For this reason, preaching can never be approached apart from the total person actually speaking.

A sermon is not just words on a page; it is sound in the air, expressions on a face, movement of the hands, the energy of a body—all channeled into a vital effort to communicate what has been experienced in the heart and understood in the mind. A preacher could spend many hours composing a literary masterpiece yet fail to move the hearts of a living audience because he read it in a dull, monotonous and detached manner. Consequently, from the very first moment of conception, the sermon, a dynamic reality, has to meet the extensive demands of oral living speech. Language, phrasing, structure and delivery must be sensitive to the varying psychological states of both the speaker and his audiences.

Insight into Meaning: The Heart of the Matter

Because preaching is the result of personally experienced theological insight into the meaning of divine revelation, two equally important elements constitute the heart of the preacher's message; if one or the other is omitted, the preaching will be ineffective. It requires the concomitant presence of both personal insight which has been theologically articulated, as well as the object of the insight, divine revelation itself.

Each sermon flows from the preacher's incisive realization of what God is telling man about Himself and man's life. The preacher's insight into the meaning of God's message brings the old revelation to new life in today's world. He articulates for his contemporaries what

God has revealed in Jesus Christ, so that they can enter into the saving action of that Gospel through faith.

The preacher, therefore, is not just dealing with facts: catechism answers, dogmatic propositions, theological definitions and moral consequences. He is totally concerned with the meaning of the facts—a meaning which has eternal consequences because each listener is personally dependent on its power for salvation and lasting happiness. Ultimately, however, the listeners can appreciate the significance of the Gospel for their lives only because the preacher has intimately grasped its significance for his own life.

The sermon, therefore, is always a breakthrough for the preacher. Its content is new and exciting because all the elements of his life have—in a flash of insight—come together in a new synthesis. Things of his life fit into the pattern of Christ's revelation that comes to us in the Scriptures. His is the "Eureka!" experience of "I understand! **That's** what it all means! Now I see what Jesus is getting at!" When everything fits together—life, experience, Scripture—the preacher is changed and his sermon is born.

Consequently, when he preaches from this insight, the preacher bears personal witness to its value. Nobody can possibly be bored by a sermon that is the result of insight, because insight is never dull. It is the light going on in the head and illuminating the heart. It is the newly-perceived idea that is relevant because it is significant. It is a "WOW!" experience because it is filled with the wonder of God.

The Academic Versus The Creative

Building sermons on personally experienced insight is difficult for many preachers because their education does not favor the development of creativity. Even before the seminary, most Americans are subject to an educational system that is primarily devoted to the acquisition of knowledge. They are formed in the order of discipline by the academic. Such formation has trained generations of students to prepare for examinations; it does not prepare them to think creatively. They learn how to assimilate information so they can answer questions about it; they do not learn how to give birth to an original idea and nurture it to maturity.

The creative act which gives birth to insight is mysterious, profound and unpredictable. Would that insight sprang full-blown from cursory contemplation! However, it is a shy child that must be coaxed from where it hides in the deepest recesses of the active mind. Study, analysis, scholarly research, exegesis, imagination—all must be used to tempt it forth into the light. Diverse elements of scripture and the contradictions of human life peek about in frustratingly playful abandon before the mind's eye, until suddenly a pattern of truth emerges, and the similarities of the dissimilar fall into an harmonious design of meaning, while randomness and obscurity give place to order and significance. In the final instant the disparate bits and pieces come together to reveal the glorious whole. That is elusive insight.

Many can be the hours spent at the desk with the Scriptures trying to pull from them an idea for a sermon, only to have absolutely nothing happen. Yet, perhaps days later, occupied in a totally unrelated task, the original struggle for meaning forgotten, suddenly the light dawns, and the sermon is born as the preacher rushes back to his desk to capture in words the insight into meaning.

In spite of the creative pain, or perhaps because of it, it is precisely these moments of insight that make the sermons such an exciting experience for the listener: he hears the mind of the preacher turning on. He sees for himself the light dawn, and he is moved to say "Amen!" That is why a sermon is life-giving, and why it is so discouraging to hear sermons which end up as simplistic, off-the-top-of-the-head, advice-giving talks. It is easy and compulsive for most humans to condemn what is wrong, particularly in a pagan world. It does not take much originality to point out the failures of society, Church or sinners, nor does it bring happiness to the hearers.

Preaching which is based on the understanding that flows from insight will always be a joy-producing experience. It will be a joy resulting from the apprehension of life-giving truth; truth which is not merely academic but creative. When the Word of God is given a home in the mind and heart of the preacher, it cannot fail to communicate itself to those to whom he speaks. As Jesus says:

> If you make my word your home
> you will indeed be my disciples,
> you will learn the truth
> and the truth
> will make you free. (Jn 8:31, 32)

The preacher who works from insight avoids a common failure: the irrelevant sermon. The irrelevant sermon produces apathy and indifference in an audience because it does not connect with their experience of life, even though it might be doctrinally accurate, even erudite. Insight, on the other hand, insures relevancy and interest because it happens only when the truth or insight is integral to the preacher's own personal existence in faith.

At the same time, a personally theological insight is not to be confused with a simple personal experience of the Lord Jesus. Such experiences are always happening to people who believe; yet, for the most part, because they remain unarticulated and unscrutinized, they are not the substance of sermons. They remain intensely private. The preacher's faith experience, however, is meant to be examined, weighed, given artistic shape and broadcast to the world at large. The focus of his preaching is not his experience of life, but the meaning of divine revelation; the focus is not the revelation of self—although that is necessarily involved—but the workings of the Divine Mind as It reaches out to caress Its creatures.

Reading the epistles of St. Paul gives us a rather intimate picture of the man, the convert and the apostle. We are admitted into the inner parts of Paul's heart and mind. We hear his boasts, learn of his weaknesses, catch glimpses of his fears and revel in his faith. Yet, for all of that, when we read his epistles, Paul leads us first and foremost to a profound and loving knowledge of Jesus Christ. Consequently, far from being anecdotal, fruitful preaching is always scriptural since it is only through the scriptures that we come to a knowledge of what the Divine Mind has revealed. Moreover, in order to penetrate into the meaning of scripture, the preacher needs to be familiar with the tools of his trade: theology, exegesis, hermeneutics and the like. The nature of the task to which he has been called demands that he become a man of the Bible, reading it constantly so that the inspired words are burned into his memory, waiting for instant recall as the need arises. Pere de Vaux, the great scripture scholar, once gave to his students the secret of penetrating into the meaning of a scriptural passage: "Read it, and read it and read it again."

It is only after laborious analysis that one can hope to achieve synthesis; consequently, it is reasonable to predict that more profound insights into the meaning of divine revelation will be the result of deeper study of scripture and theology.

Simple and Direct

Because a sermon is an oral communication, it should be modeled on the qualities of vital conversation. Indeed it is a kind of conversation—a dialogue between two people: the preacher and his listener, whether it be one, a hundred or a thousand; we listen in groups but we respond individually. The listener may never voice his thoughts, but as the preacher talks, he is responding internally: asking questions, making comments, agreeing or arguing. The skillful preacher, recognizing this process, seeks to anticipate the mental activities of his listener so that the process of mutual understanding leads to agreement and sharing of meaning. Preaching involves two minds trying to come together as one; consequently, no ornamental flourishes should be added to complicate the process or impede the union.

On the contrary, the effective sermon is marked by simplicity of expression and directness of thought. It is not a literary masterpiece to be read and savored at leisure. It is a passing moment of insight, directed at human beings whose imaginations are teeming with images and whose minds are torn apart with distractions. Yet, when it breaks through all the barriers of time, place and person, it can bring the listener to a new knowledge of Jesus Christ. Nothing can surpass simple, sincere, direct human contact for accomplishing that.

It is particularly true today, exposed as we are to the intensely personal medium of television, that literary pretensions and rhetorical efforts should be avoided. Rather, the key to organizing a sermon is to have a point and to get to it quickly. In times past, preachers were taught that each sermon should consist of an introduction, body and conclusion. Although this structural pattern is no longer generally taught, a common impediment to effective preaching is still the search for a gripping introduction. Some preachers spend so much time introducing their sermon that by the time they get to their point, they do not have enough time to develop it adequately. As a result, even if the point is grasped, it will not be remembered. Most preachers could take the first nine minutes and thirty seconds of a ten-minute sermon and throw it away, because so frequently it is only in the last thirty seconds that they come to the point. Had they started with it, they would have been able to develop it into an effective communication of God's word.

Development is crucial to understanding the point and appreciating its ramifications, and the key to development is focus, the sharper the better. The preacher asks, "What do I want to say?" then says it directly, illustrating it and exemplifying it. Explanation alone is usually dull; development requires narrative that involves the audience's ordinary experiences, and excites their emotions as they grasp the significance of the truth being revealed.

Unfortunately, many preachers, because they do not adequately prepare, use valuable time in the act of preaching trying to come up with a point. Unprepared sermons are characterized by rambling, as the preacher throws a series of unconnected ideas out into the void with the hope that by the time he is finished something will have stuck with someone. One preacher, after a particularly rambling presentation, remarked to his audience, "I think there was a point in all that." The need for sharp focus—a sermon should have a point—is so obvious that having to treat it as a serious problem in contemporary preaching is the best indicator of the need for renewal. For the tragic truth is, most sermons ramble.

On the assumption, however, that there is a point to be developed, development always takes place in the light of the audience to whom it is addressed: their needs, experience and state of mind and heart. Relevancy is best assured when the preacher answers within the first thirty seconds of his sermon the sub-conscious question on the minds of his listeners: "So what?" A preacher can expound the greatest truth, the most profound insight, the most important idea, but unless the listener understands how it relates to him personally, he simply does not listen.

In fact, Americans have become adept at not listening. They are practiced at "turning off" the irrelevant. The greatest non-listeners in the world spent their childhood (and in some cases, even their young adulthood) learning not to listen—in the classroom. Boredom is the occupational hazard of the student, but its debilitating effects on the psyche are considerably lessened when the mind is allowed to wander as the dulling voice of useless information drones on. To break into that habitual pattern of listening, each sermon must connect immediately with the needs of the audience. The great speech teacher Alan H. Monroe, and his colleague, Douglas Ehninger, put it this way in their excellent book, **Principles and Types of Speech,** (Scott, Foresman & Co., Sixth Edition, 1976):

A speaker cannot ram ideas down people's throats. Instead of trying to force his listeners to conclusions against their wills, he must lead their thinking so that they will respond in a way in accord with his specific purpose. To succeed in this undertaking, the speaker must build his speech with his audience constantly in mind and must plan the structure of his speech so that its sequence of points corresponds to the way people habitually arrive at understanding or belief or a decision to act. (p. 264)

The Gospel has to be heard before it can be believed. Its

ideas have to be grasped, their import understood before a faith decision can be rendered. Indifference is not a response to the word of God; apathy means the message has not gotten through. When the listener has heard the word, some kind of positive response will occur: either outright rejection or complete acceptance, or, as in the case of most human reactions, a period of weighing, considering, deciding before a final judgment is rendered. Preaching has a cumulative effect. This means that not every sermon will change everybody's life immediately, but it can be one of the building blocks that, over a long period of time, and in accord with God's mercy, will lead to change and salvation through faith.

The Work of the Spirit

God's mercy is the final element in preaching since preaching is always the work of the Spirit. In times past, the question that provoked much theological discussion was, "What kind of causality does the act of preaching exercise on the hearer?" St. Thomas Aquinas, for example, opted for preachings being only a dispositive cause of faith in the order of material causality. (De Veritate, q. 27, art. 3, ad. 12)

Without reviving that kind of theological reflection now, it is the clear teaching of Sacred Scripture that it is the preaching of the Word of God that brings faith to those who hear. Unless there is preaching, there is no faith. We cannot know Jesus Christ except through the word which reveals Him. We cannot hear the word of Christ except from the lips of those whom He has sent. (Rom 10:14-17) St. Paul stresses the power of the word when he says: "I am not ashamed of the Good News; it is the power of God saving all who have faith." (Rom 1:16) St. Peter reinforces this teaching of Paul when he writes:

Your new birth was not from any mortal seed
but from the everlasting word of the living
and eternal God. What is this word? It is
the Good News that has been brought to you.
(1 P 1:23)

Kinds of Preaching

In the Roman Catholic tradition there has been such
a blurring of the general concept of preaching that there
is little practical appreciation for the necessity of divid-
ing preaching into three distinct categories each with
its own characteristics, its own purposes and its own
limitations. Preaching in general is not an operative reality; there are only sermons which have specific purposes
and meet specific needs. No single sermon format or
series of formats encompass all that preaching is capable
of doing to beget and nourish faith in Jesus Christ. Yet,
for most preachers and people, preaching has come to
mean only pulpit preaching, especially the Sunday homily. And the Sunday homily has come to mean only moral
applications of gospel truths. So far had the Sunday
sermon fallen in the esteem of the Church before the
Second Vatican Council that it was regarded as an inter-
ruption, although legitimate, in the Sacrifice of the Mass
and ranked in dignity down with candles and vestments.

Renewal in preaching, therefore, calls for basic
changes in the way preacher and people think about
preaching. If it is truly a principal duty of bishops, priests
and, indeed, the entire People of God, preaching should
become a real priority in the life of the Church requiring
a major expenditure of effort and time in the formation
of preachers and the exercise of the ministry itself as
part of parish life.

A beginning in the renewal of thought and attitudes
about preaching might also be made by identifying the

unique characteristics of the various kinds of preaching so that the special powers of each may be fully utilized in the communication of the Good News. For, while the characteristics of preaching outlined in the preceding pages, especially the importance of theological insight into its scriptural base, are common attributes of all the preaching the Church undertakes, theology also distinguishes three kinds of preaching by reason of the kind of faith it engenders.

Evangelization, or kerygmatic preaching, is directed towards the non-believer and leads him to an initial act of faith — conversion. **Catechesis,** the second kind of preaching, presupposes initial faith in the heart of the listener and, while deepening it, forms the reborn in the Christian living out of the faith. Thirdly, **didascalia** brings the formed, mature believer into the fullest union with God through the revelation of the deepest mysteries of His immanence and transcendence.

The form each of these kinds of preaching takes will vary from informal conversation to a highly structured liturgical homily or religious education presentation. The organization of the material is not, however, the distinguishing mark of the preaching genre; that mark is scriptural content in relation to the listener.

CHAPTER TWO

EVANGELIZATION

Pre-Evangelization

Religious educators seem to agree that in order for a person to be able to hear the gospel and to accept Jesus Christ as Lord and Saviour, he has to be living a basically human existence. In the material order, he has to have the basic necessities of life: food, clothing, shelter. In addition, they cite as prerequisites for conversion certain spiritual qualities, for example, the ability to grasp the nature of spiritual reality, the possession of a sense of personal worth, a sense of the mystery of what is beyond him, and above all, a recognition of the helplessness of man and the need of salvation. Until these conditions are present in the life of a person, they say, he cannot actually hear the word of God in a way that leads to faith.

Without arguing the merits of this opinion, and while admitting that tragically in many parts of the world basic needs are not being met and fundamental spiritual qualities are lacking, there is no question that they are present in the vast majority of the people of the United States who enjoy the highest standard of living in the history of the world, and who possess an educational system which effectively forms the qualities that are necessary to be evangelized.

There is no further need to lay the groundwork for the gospel through pre-evangelization in the United

States; it has already been done. The conditions required for conversion are already present in our cultural, social and economic life, so that we need only the vigorous, explicit and faith-filled proclamation of the Good News. Christians fail the Gospel when they fail to preach Christ explicitly as Saviour, and the seriousness of their failure to obey the gospel mandate becomes apparent when even the most conservative estimates indicate that 80 million Americans belong to no church, and therefore must be numbered among those who have not yet "called upon the name of the Lord to be saved." (Rom 10:13)

Given the fact that the people of the United States are adequately prepared to hear the Gospel at this time, how does one proclaim Christ? Where does one start? This is the work of evangelization.

The Conversion Experience

Evangelical preaching proclaims the word of God to those who either have not yet heard it, or have not yet believed it. Evangelization leads to conversion, to **metanoia.** Metanoia is not just a sorrow for past sins that the English translation "repentance" might imply, nor is it merely the acquisition of academic knowledge about Christ. Metanoia is a total change of heart which results in the radical restructuring of one's whole life in the light of new gospel power and values. Conversion gives the believer new goals to achieve and the power to achieve them. In the light of these goals, he sets new priorities and undertakes new activities. The experience of conversion is one of stepping out from the darkness of despair into the brightness of the light of Christ. Far more than gaining new information about Christ, the converted person actually comes into Christ's presence as he is reborn in the Spirit and lives by this life-giving principle. Evangelization, therefore, is the absolute starting point of Christianity. It begins when the Good News is heard and believed, and the heart opened by Divine Love.

It is obvious that there can be knowledge of Christ and His teachings without belief in Him as Lord and Saviour. One can have gone through many years of Catholic religious education, learned the catechism and recited its answers, received the sacraments and still not have believed; know intellectually and yet not have had one's life really transformed by the joy and peace that comes from experiencing the exercise of Christ's lordship and love. (Mt 11:28; Ph 4:4-6) Quite the contrary, information alone about religion can create an aversion to it since, while its demands are clearly perceived, the divine power by which the demands can be met is not experienced. The sense of failure and inadequacy that results causes discouragement, not joy; frustration, not freedom. Guilt without redemption brings death to the human spirit.

Conversion may take place in a sudden blinding flash of realization and illumination, like Paul on the road to Damascus, and there are many today who can testify to the very hour of their "rebirth." On the other hand, it may be so gradual over a long period of time that no one incident stands out as decisive. The latter is particularly true of people who have "been born into the faith."

Nevertheless, whether startling in its inception or not, conversion is a continuing process of growth in the new way of life, and continues as long as the believer dies anew each day to sin and self, as God's redeeming love drives out sin, enlightens the mind and makes the child of God holy.

Because there are always remnants of the pagan in the flesh of man, there is no time in the lives of believers when the proclamation of the kerygma becomes superfluous. It is the kerygma which gives birth to the faith that leads to salvation, and so believers need to hear it again and again, adapted to meet new conditions of existence to bring them into fresh contact with Jesus Christ as Saviour and Lord.

The Content of Evangelization

The events of Christ's coming into the world to bring salvation to sinners constitute the content of evangelization. Called the **kerygma,** (a Greek word for what a herald proclaims) the trumpeting of Christ's birth, death, resurrection and ascension into heaven is the starting point of the Christian Gospel. Born of a woman, Jesus was a man who lived at a certain time, in a particular country—a historical figure; yet, the knowledge the believer has of Jesus is as the Christ, the Saviour of mankind. Although historical, the kerygma is more than history; it is the divine interpretation of the words, events and persons God uses to bring rescue to those whom He has chosen.

The apostles were the first preachers of the kerygma, and evidences of their charismatic preaching are found throughout the New Testament. Probably the five discourses of Peter in the **Acts of the Apostles** and the discourse of Paul in Chapter 13 are simply the summary of the kind of preaching done by all the apostolic witnesses which forms the basic plan of all four Gospels. The proclamation of the same kerygma today gives birth to faith and leads the hearers to the person of Jesus Christ.

In other words, the Church does not simply pass on information about a dead hero who lived in the distant past; rather, through the words of Scripture coming alive in its preachers, the Church brings men and women into union with the living Jesus, who is eternally with the Father, exercising his Lordship over all creation. Today's preacher, like the apostles before him, bears witness to the transcendent nature of the person of Jesus because the preacher has also experienced His saving action in his own life. Like all Christians, preachers have been given the Holy Spirit Who makes Christ present to all ages; He is the source of their power to preach.

Because of the Holy Spirit, the preacher is able to proclaim a divine history that has been made his own, and in which he is an active participant. There is none of the objective detachment of the secular historian for the man of faith! The Christian preacher is there; he speaks out of the urgency of one who sees, tastes, feels; he broadcasts the truth because he has experienced the truth personally in his own life. Having been brought himself from darkness to light through Jesus Christ, he preaches the kerygma out of the perspective of what Jesus is doing for him personally in the present, as well as what he did in the distant past. Past and present, therefore, are one in the life experience of the chosen witness—the preacher—who lives today in the continuing context of the past.

Just as Paul proclaimed the faith out of his weakness, and Peter preached as one who had been forgiven, so the preacher of today bears witness as a sinner who has been saved. The example that he offers to the world to justify its listening to his message is that of a happy man revealing the source of his happiness, Jesus Christ.

This understanding of kerygmatic preaching can keep the contemporary evangelizer from falling into that offensive self-righteousness so characteristic of the proselytizer, who seeks to ram down the throats of his audience (frequently captive) his own peculiar ideological, sociological or ethical principles. While such proselytizing is justifiably resented by those who are subjected to it, it is difficult to see how anyone could resent a person's sharing the most intimate and fulfilling experience of happiness that he has ever had—the presence of Jesus Christ in his life as friend, saviour and Lord.

The Fulfillment of Prophecy

Evangelization begins with the announcement that the last days foretold by the prophets of the Old Testament have begun. Jesus does not just unexpectedly appear on the scene claiming to be Son of God—out of the blue, as it were. His coming into history was prepared for by history when God sent certain chosen persons to prophesy that Jesus would be born, suffer, die and be raised from the dead. God spent generations preparing His people, Israel, to welcome that promised Messiah who would save them from their sins. Historical events shaped their national destiny: wars, plagues, wanderings, exile and return. The prophets, acting as agents of God, interpreted the meaning of these events so that when the fulness of time came, the Chosen People might be ready to hear the news of Jesus' coming with faith and greet Him with repentence and joy. The long line of prophets culminated in the ministry of John the Baptist, and altogether their testimony is weighty evidence for the authenticity of Jesus' Messiahship. His Gospel, therefore, is not merely uplifting legend; it is historical truth that God has intervened decisively and powerfully in the affairs of men.

In His earthly ministry, all the things that the prophets said would happen to Jesus happened to Him; however, they are not known to us from just historical sources immediately and directly. They are mediated to us by a believing community who, after Jesus' resurrection, continued to experience and celebrate His presence among them. At the same time, because the early Christians were filled with the Holy Spirit, they could look back into the historical past when Jesus walked the earth before His death and understand His teaching and His person in a way that made them appreciate the greatness of the gift God had given them in His Son. The mystery of the Cross was revealed in the glory of the Resurrection.

Consequently, the four gospels that have been handed down to us in the Church as the inspired word of God reflect the different conditions that exist in the community celebrating the life of Christ at the time the different gospels were written. The Gospel according to Mark, for example, emphasizes Jesus as the Suffering Servant, hiding His Messiahship from those who are unappreciative of its significance and revealing it only to His chosen disciples, and even at that it was a revelation that was met with misunderstanding. It reflects, perhaps, an effort on the part of the Church to counteract a Christianity which expected too much immediate satisfaction and dwelt excessively on the present joy of the Good News.

The Gospel according to Luke reflects a tradition and communal celebration more attuned to the Divine Drama of which Jesus is the Hero. The subtleties of Jewish practices have been laid aside, and the universal appeal of His message, and the general attractiveness of His person, are presented in a way which even non-Jews can appreciate and identify with. The Gospel according to Matthew sees Jesus as the fulfillment of the Law of Moses, for the community at the time of its writing was still struggling with the relationship between the New and Old Law, seeking to harmonize them yet preserving the clear eminence of Jesus as the Christ.

The life, ministry, death and resurrection of Jesus, therefore, comes to us not simply through historical validation, but through faith. It is only through faith that we can come to an understanding of His life and death and, thereby, come to the saving experience of

Jesus as Lord. So if faith was important for the early Christian to know Jesus, it is equally important for the preacher today. When he proclaims the resurrection, he proclaims it out of his own faith-experience. He can bear witness to its truth because he has experienced its fruits in his own life, just as the early communities did. History limits us to an empty tomb; only faith can take us beyond the tomb to the reality that the tomb was empty because Jesus rose from the dead.

The proclamation of the Gospel Message even when limited to Christ's earthly ministry, therefore, is not something which is centered in the past; it is present in the preacher's life as well, and his preaching, like the preaching of the early Church, will reflect his own pilgrimage of faith as he comes to grips with the Mystery that has been revealed. At different times he will emphasize different aspects of the Gospel as they touch more intimately into the core of his own existence. Consequently, the preaching of the kerygma can never be routine instruction in the basic truths of the faith. It is never the mere recounting of historical facts, for the proclamation of the kerygma always requires that the preacher bring to bear the testimony of his own experience, in the Spirit, of the events of Christ's life as they touch him through faith. Always, however, Scripture is the norm for the validation of his experience of Jesus.

Resurrection and Exaltation

By virtue of His resurrection, Jesus has been raised up to sit at the right head of God. This popular and vivid scriptural image is obscure to those unfamiliar with the ways of kings. It seeks to convey the reality that Jesus has completed his earthly work and now enjoys forever the fruits of His labors. He has power and rule; He is happy and content; He is secure in honor, and He is equal with the Father as God and pre-eminent among men as Man. As a result of Jesus' being so exalted, God's saving action is not limited to Israel and the historical; it reaches beyond time and space; it fills all creation, reaching up to the very throne of God Himself. It unites all in One, since Jesus reigns as the Head of the New Israel, embracing all nations and all generations.

Christian faith, therefore, is not just a call for moral living on earth leading to peace, justice and love among men. Faith leads to glory—the sharp, clear knowledge of God and being known by God; it is a knowledge which is coupled with honor and praise, radiance and joy; it is a knowledge which begins now and never ends.

> God raised him high
> and gave him the name
> which is above all other names,
> so that all beings
> in the heavens, on earth, and in the underworld
> should bend the knee at the name of Jesus
> and that every tongue should acclaim
> Jesus Christ as Lord
> to the glory of God the Father. (Ph 2:10 ff).

The kerygmatic content of evangelistic preaching is not concerned with memories of times past. Quite the contrary, its whole thrust is concern for the present; not mere events, but power and glory. Only glory could have driven the martyrs to the extremes of witness they endured, and only power could have sustained them in their sufferings. In the agony of his cruel stoning, Scripture says:

> Steven, filled with the Holy Spirit, gazed
> into the heavens and saw the glory of God and

Jesus, standing at God's right hand. "I can
see heaven thrown open," he said, "and the
son of man standing at the right hand of God!"
(Ac 7:55 ff.)

The book of Revelation was written for Christians
who were losing sight of the transcendent quality of
their faith because the coming of Jesus was delayed and
their persecution was growing. All the brilliant and
mysterious images that are used in that book made vivid
to a people caught up in the sufferings of earth the
realities which are beyond the earth. Both their trials
and their liturgies were reflections of heavenly realities.
Their ordinary Sunday and daily worship, their gathering around the Eucharist of the Lord, the hymns they
sang, the praises they offered, even if done in secret and
paid for by their own blood, reached to the Court of
Heaven and became one with the acclamations of the
Heavenly Hosts. Although still in time, they reached into
eternity.

Unless the preacher can communicate something of
the vitality of that heavenly vision, his preaching will
not be effective in proclaiming the reality of earthly
faith. "If our hope in Christ has been for this life only,
we are the most unfortunate of all people." (1 Cor 15:19)
With that vision his words bring his hearers beyond the
grave to glory.

Personal Transformation

Although the Christian is destined for glory, and his
faith reaches out beyond time to eternity, he is also
thoroughly a creature of this world. Jesus did not preach
an escapist philosophy simply to enable His followers
to endure the hardships of life. The Christian does not
aim for a distant ideal; he transforms the real by what

he does as a result of being moved by the Holy Spirit. So no matter how transcendent the Christian religion, it is also intensely personal.

Indeed, it is the personal transformation of its members, either in wonderful signs of tongues, prophecies, healings, or an equally wonderful life of holiness, generosity and service that is the great sign of the Church's authenticity as a construct of God. The Church is its members, and its members are Christ, living by the Holy Spirit and loving with the love of God Himself.

To appreciate what it means to love with the love of God Himself takes a lifetime of personal growth in both understanding Christian revelation and actually loving: self, others, God. Unfortunately, to "love with the love of God Himself" can remain empty words; the preacher's task is to open up the dimensions of that expression into an experienced reality.

The result, however, of this on-going experience of divine love is a personal transformation. Through love, God's love in him, the believer is delivered from slavery to sin and the unhappiness which is its fruit and given instead the open-ended gifts of freedom, joy and peace. It is this personal transformation of the believer which is a testimony to both men and angels that God is Love.

Furthermore, God has chosen this time to manifest to all creation the extent of His glory and power through the final unfolding of the divine plan. His wisdom is now fully revealed in Christ Jesus, both in His exaltation from the death on the Cross to the right hand of the Father, and in His continuing presence in the gathering of all those who believe in Him. Immanence and transcendence are the constituent thrusts of the Christian faith; without one or the other the message is not the truth that makes man free. The realization of the power of the gospel message does not have to be postponed to a vague eschatology in a distant heaven, for now in the Church is the time, now in our lives is the day of salvation.

The preacher's own act of ministry is itself the fruit of his personal transformation by the Spirit in his own life and in the life of the Church as a whole. Paul, in discussing the difference between the Old and New Covenants, points out that his qualifications to preach come from God through the Spirit when he says:

> He is the one who has given us the quali-
> fications to be the administrators of
> this new covenant, which is not a covenant
> of written letters but of the Spirit; the
> written letters bring death, but the Spirit
> gives life. (2 Cor 3:6)

Later on, Paul emphasizes that without the personal transformation that God's love brings, the preacher is simply a "gong booming or a cymbal clashing." (1 Cor 13:1) Thus, Christian fruitfulness is always the consequence of a personal transformation brought about by the Spirit and intended as the authentic sign of God's operating graciousness.

The Return of Christ

While the kerygma, which the preacher proclaims, reveals that the Messianic Age has already begun, it is by no means the end. The outpouring of the Spirit into the hearts of believers in this world results in joy, peace and love that is difficult to describe. Yet, the life of the Spirit here is only a faint reflection of the glory that is still to come. For this age is destined to attain a fullness and an attendant splendor in the return of Christ that human beings cannot even imagine, let alone put into words:

Things that no eye has seen and no ear
has heard, things beyond the mind of man, all
that God has prepared for those who love him.
(1 Cor 2:9)

The ultimate state to which Christians aspire is not
a world of peace and justice that is still subject to death
and decay; Christians yearn for things beyond the mere
reorganization of human society and the making of a
better place on earth in which to live. Even Utopia would
only be a stopping point on the way to a better and
eternal land.

For us, our homeland is in Heaven. And
from heaven comes the Saviour we are waiting
for, the Lord Jesus Christ. And he will
transfigure these wretched bodies of ours
into copies of his glorious body. And he
will do that by the same power with which he
subdues the whole universe. (Ph 3:20)

So fulfilling will that coming of Christ be, when all things
are set right and death will be no more, that the scripture writers can only describe it in apocalyptic terms.
They conjure up violent images of cataclysmic change
which shakes the very foundations of the universe and
catches up every human being who has ever lived in vast
upheaval which will make everything totally new.

The study of the Second Coming is a fascinating one,
as scripture scholars and theologians are discovering
today in their re-examination of the meaning of the
images used by the sacred writers. John's understanding
of the Second Coming of Christ seems different from that
of the synoptics, and Paul's thought evolves considerably
from what he taught in his early epistles, such as Thessa-
lonians, to his more mature reflections in his later works.

Although the theological explanations of the Second Coming—within Scripture and outside it—vary considerably, the fact that there will be a return of Christ in fullness, power and majesty to take up all those who call upon His name, is of the heart of the kerygma and not an optional appendix. Christ's Kingdom is not of this world, and in order to be fully in His Kingdom, His followers will be transported to a new reality the existence of which they can only take on faith.

Repent

When the glories promised by the kerygma are heard and believed, there can be only one response for those who are chosen—to change in order to receive. Consequently, also at the heart of the initial announcement of the Christian gospel is the appeal for repentance. However, repentance in the gospel sense is not the same as what the English term commonly means. To repent is not just to be sorry for sin, a regret over things that were done in the past; rather, to repent is to reorder one's priorities in the light of the promises and the glory revealed in the kerygma and thus to establish a new way of life with new goals and new values. To repent is to acquire a new mind set, an attitude which is so radically holy that it is identified with the mind of Christ Himself.

The evangelist, therefore, does not settle for intellectual agreement with certain propositional truths about the nature of God, man and the universe; he holds out the rich promises of the kerygma as he seeks a personal commitment on the part of each one of his hearers to worship the Father through Christ Jesus. He does not settle for a political vote on social or economic issues; he calls for a change of heart and mind. He offers his hearers a new way of life that will extend beyond the grave itself:

You must give up your old way of life,
you must put aside your old self which gets
corrupted by following illusory desires.
Your mind must be renewed by a spiritual
revolution so that you can put on the new
self which has been created in God's way,
in goodness and holiness of the truth. (Ep 4:22-24)

The demand for change which is inherent in the gospel message can be made for two reasons; first, the glory that results is worth the sacrifice involved, and secondly, the Gospel itself gives the power to effect the change it demands. The scriptures sum up this relationship when Paul writes to the Colossians:

Since you have been brought back to true
life with Christ, you must look for the things
which are in heaven, where Christ is sitting
at God's right hand. Let your thoughts be on
heavenly things, not on things that are of earth,
because you have died and now the life you have
is hidden with Christ in God. But when Christ is
revealed—and He is your life—you too will be
revealed in all your glory with him. (Col 3:1-4)

Because faith effects change, the preacher reveals the way the change will take place by the power of the Spirit. In a certain sense, the preacher can be said to "demand" change; but it is unreasonable to demand change without the giving of life through faith. Unfortunately, today the experience of many who hear Christian preaching is that the preacher starts commanding and demanding before he gives the promises; he looks for obedience to faith without first giving the substance of faith. He offers advice instead of salvation, moralization in place of evangelization.

Today, from what religious publications are saying, there are many Christians who are shocked at the rising figures of abortion, crime, promiscuity, divorce and other failures of human beings; yet, shock and dismay are inappropriate responses for believers, since they indicate that these Christians expect pagans to be able to act like Christians and achieve moral perfection on their own—by their own will power and in the light of their own human wisdom—without faith. It is American optimism transferred to the religious sphere: man is innately good and needs only the right environment to achieve his full potential. Such an attitude overlooks the reality of sin, a power which has weakened man both intellectually and volitionally, and left him in need of healing.

Even Christians, given the grace of God and the outpouring of the Spirit, are still subject to sin; salvation is not fully completed in this life, but whatever goodness is achieved is due to the utter gratuity of God's boundless mercy. To be shocked by sin in self or others is a sign that this gratuity of salvation is not fully appreciated but is experienced instead as merely one of life's many options for good and evil.

While great energies are being spent today on legislative reform and political action, as yet the basic ministry of evangelization is being sadly neglected. However, the mere passage of laws does not change hearts, and the reconstruction of the social order does not bring salvation; only Jesus can do that. When we believe in Him, the power of God that raised Jesus from the dead changes our desires and loves and moves us to think creatively in a way which enables us to reach our new goals. The pagan is unable to escape from his own vain illusion and the weakness of his vacillating will; consequently, he is filled with frustration and despair which, as rising figures indicate, frequently leads to suicide.

When you were slaves of sin, you felt no
obligation to righteousness and what did you
get from this? Nothing but experiences that
now make you blush, since that sort of
behavior ends in death. Now, however, you
have been set free from sin, you have been
made slaves to God and you get a reward
leading to your sanctification and ending
in eternal life. For the wage paid by sin
is death; the present given by God is eternal
life in Christ Jesus our Lord. (Rm 6:20-23)

The Promise of Forgiveness

Guilt is a reality of human experience; rightly, or
perhaps at times wrongly, we feel guilty about things
we have done or failed to do. Unrelieved guilt can be a
soul-destroying experience that saps spiritual strength
and imprisons the guilty in a world of endless regret. It
gives birth to a sadness that prevents any effort at creative out-reach so that he is cut off from the nourishment
of normal human relationships. Guilt can lead to madness, as the Psalmist says:

Some, driven frantic by their sins,
made miserable by their own guilt
and finding all food repugnant,
were nearly at death's door. (Ps 107:17)

One of the great promises that the kerygma offers the
believer is that however he has failed in the past, the
fault is wiped away by God's mercy. Fear and anxiety—
the nameless dread of future retribution as the past
catches up with the guilty—are cast aside by the profound experience of the constant presence of God. With
utmost confidence the Christian can look to the future

because the future is one of a life changed and redirected. The moral failings and the weaknesses of the past, crimes of malice as well as passion, cannot undermine the endeavors of the new life in Christ.

The Christian who, on the evidence of his past failures, cannot trust himself does, as a result of faith, trust God. Enlightened by the Spirit, he realizes that God can accomplish, even in a sinner like himself, what he alone can never do. So while sin may still be at work in the convert, God's power is even more in evidence, and the experience of the divine power destroying, perhaps slowly, the ramparts of sin, fills the soul of the believer with a peace that is itself testimony to the operation of God's salvation.

> Having died to make us righteous, is it
> likely that he would now fail to save us from
> God's anger? When we were reconciled to God
> by the death of his son, we were still
> enemies; now that we have been reconciled,
> surely we may count on being saved by the life
> of his son. Not merely because we have been
> reconciled, but because we are filled with
> a joyful trust in God, through our Lord Jesus
> Christ, through whom we have already gained
> our reconciliation. (Rm 5:10-11)

Unredeemed guilt is a terrible burden that, without Christ, man must bear alone. It is not to be wondered, then, that rebirth through faith brings with it a tremendous feeling of relief, escape and oneness with all creation. Above all, forgiveness brings with it reconciliation with God and man, renewed awareness of solidarity that extends even to one's former victims. Such a transforming experience of deliverance is a great incentive for the sinner to trust his Deliverer in all things, confident that He will provide, as Romans teaches, all that is needful for a holy life in His presence and love.

Nor is the confidence the believer feels upon deliverance from sin limited to the sphere of inner feelings alone. The Gospel promises that all the material needs of the believer as well will be met by the Father Who works out all things for his good. Indeed, Jesus insists that confidence in His Father for even the mundane material necessities of life was to characterize his followers. He says:

> You must not set your hearts on things
> to eat and things to drink, nor must you worry.
> It is the pagans of this world who set their
> hearts on all these things. Your Father well
> knows you need them. No, set your hearts on
> His kingdom, and these other things will be
> given you as well. There is no need to be afraid,
> little flock, it has pleased your Father to give
> you the Kingdom. (Lk 12:29 ff)

It is because he is being provided for by a generous and bountiful Father that the Christian can embrace voluntary poverty so readily. In the past, voluntary poverty has found expression in the communal possession of goods by the first Christians, and by long monastic and mendicant traditions in religious congregations of the Roman Catholic Church. These manifestations of confidence which are fundamental to the Christian faith are still being practiced today by believers who put their hopes not in wealth, insurance or lucrative jobs, but in the unseen realities revealed by the Holy Spirit.

Nevertheless, since poverty and a spirit of trusting detachment are effects of faith, they cannot be imposed. They are matters of the heart which has been touched by the Spirit, and consequently, each believer will respond in his own way to the demands of the Gospel for poverty, detachment and trust as the Spirit gives him the will to respond. The preacher, therefore, always respects the freedom of each to fulfill his vocation in the Lord as he proclaims the promise.

Eternal Life

Flesh is the breeding place of sorrow, and the joy of the faith does not, in this life, end suffering and death, although suffering and pain are eased when they are made meaningful through faith. The kerygma tells those who enter the elect community, the Church, through faith in Jesus Christ that their sufferings are now united to the sufferings of Christ on His cross and, therefore, they enjoy the sure knowledge and firm hope that what they endure on earth is preparing them for eternal life in heaven.

St. Paul uses a wonderful image to describe how the sufferings of this life strengthen the Christian for the life that is to come and that will be without end. The Christian on earth is like a weightlifter who is preparing for a championship match. He goes through a daily grind of lifting ever-increasing weights until he is strong enough to lift the great weight of the championship contest. So, too, the Christian lifts the light weights of suffering in this world, and these prepare him to lift and bear forever the eternal weight of God's glory—in Hebrew the divine **Kadosh**.

That is why there is no weakening on our part, and instead, though this outer man of ours may be falling into decay, the inner man is renewed day by day. Yes, the troubles which are soon over, though they weigh little, train

us for the carrying of a weight of eternal
glory which is out of all proportion to them.
(2 Cor 4:16-18)

With entrance into the Church of Christ, the believer
has poured out upon him the power of God, shaping,
molding, forgiving, strengthening. He does not just hope
blindly for something that is to come, because in the
depths of his heart he is already experiencing the glory-
that-is-to-come in the form of a first installment. Sufferings, thereby, are transformed, and sorrow gives place
to joy because of the sure promise that we will live forever in Christ Jesus our Lord.

Everyone moved by the Spirit is a son of God.
The Spirit we received is not the spirit of
slaves bringing fear into your lives again;
it is the spirit of sons, and it makes us
cry, 'Abba, Father.' The Spirit himself and
our spirit bear united witness that we are the
children of God, and if we are children we are
heirs as well—heirs of God and co-heirs with
Christ, sharing his sufferings so as to share
his glory. (Rm 8:14)

The Kerygma: The Absolute Starting Point

Although the preaching of the kerygma alone can
bring about conversion of life which leads to happiness,
its truth cannot be proven by rational argument. The
kerygma is proclaimed to be believed, and everything
that Christians are and do depends on their acceptance
of the kerygma and their faith in Jesus Christ as Lord
and Saviour.

Christianity, therefore, at its core is not new demands,

challenges or commitments; it is new life. The re-born Christian lives out the good news that God is rescuing the believer from sin through His Son, Jesus Christ. The Saviour is freeing him from all that holds him prisoner, delivering him from illusions that lead to death. The salvation which is being given him is verified by the profound experience of interior peace, personal happiness and a new sense of identity and purpose.

There is much evidence to indicate that the kerygma is rarely preached today except in "convert" classes. For the most part, preachers assume that the events of the kerygma are known, understood, and above all, believed by those who profess to be Christians. The kerygma seems to have become superfluous. However, since conversion is not a once-in-a-lifetime event, but rather an on-going process lasting a whole lifetime, it is necessary that the events which brought and bring faith into existence are presented again and again, in a new way, under a new light, as the preacher experiences for himself in different ways their truth and power. The kerygma, should always be a regular part of Sunday preaching.

The construction of Paul's epistles show the intimate connection between faith and action, kerygma and morality, for Paul always connects his exhortations for Christian living and his specific directives for community life to the doctrinal and kerygmatic truths which form their basis. He does not assume faith in his converts, he proclaims endlessly the Good News which begets faith. Without the proclamation of the kerygma in his sermons, the preacher of today can rapidly fall into being simply a giver of good advice, but not the bringer of Good News, and it is the Good News, after all, which is the power of God.

Pope Paul VI's **Apostolic Exhortation on Evangelization in the Modern World** has revived intense interest in evangelization after centuries of neglect. As a result of neglect, the theological substratum for effective evangelization is so weak that some try to make evangelization include everything the Church does. It is important to realize, therefore, that as fundamental as evangelization is, it is only one of the many ministries of the Church. Rather than forcing evangelization to include everything that is being done today, new priorities of pastoral action should be established which respect its specific qualities and provide for their most fruitful expression.

It is of particular importance that on-going programs in evangelization be inaugurated on both diocesan and parish levels. (Simply put, dioceses and parishes should drastically increase the number of adult baptisms into the faith.) Since evangelization is not just another program but the basic purpose of the Church, evangelization should be an important part of all religious education curricula for both children and adults. It should constitute a significant part of priestly formation, especially through pastoral training programs. In this way, evangelization will once again become integral to the ordinary Christian experience. It will be the inevitable consequence of the experience of salvation and the result of an unflagging desire to share the Good News with all creation.

CHAPTER THREE

CATECHESIS

Building on Conversion

Catechesis is the second kind of preaching. Directed to the listener who has heard the kerygma and has accepted Jesus Christ as Lord and Saviour, catechetical preaching builds on evangelization by showing the believer how to live out his new life in Christ which began with his conversion. The conversion to belief which makes it possible for the listener to be catechized may occur suddenly in adult life even in a recognizable and recallable moment so that the convert can truly speak of an experience of "being reborn" (Jn 3:3)—the vivid and lasting Damascus Road experience of St. Paul. On the other hand, conversion may be a life-long process that began at the mother's knee and was nourished by family love, childhood prayer, bedtime Bible stories, and a Catholic or Church education. Such a process of conversion may be so long, so gradual and so deep-seated that while high and low moments of faith are experienced, no single incident can be isolated as "the moment of re-birth."

Whichever occurs, it nonetheless remains true that conversion to Jesus is necessary before effective catechetical preaching is possible and the word of God can bear fruit in terms of shaping the Christian life. At some point, moreover, no matter how quietly, this conversion must become an adult experience; that is, at whatever age it is made, the believer must "knowingly, freely, and gratefully" accept the Lordship of Jesus as his Saviour. In the Roman tradition, such an adult decision is recognized as possible at seven, the age of reason, when the child is considered capable of distinguishing serious right, serious wrong and of making a choice.

Formation for Worship

The quality that ultimately characterizes the life of the converted Christian is worship. Having experienced the saving power of Jesus Christ in his life, the Christian devotes all his energies, his powers, his life itself to giving thanks and praise for having been the recipient of God's totally unmerited mercy. Catechesis reveals how the Christian does this.

St. Paul catechizes when he says:

Think of God's mercy, my brothers, and
worship Him I beg you in a way that is worthy
of thinking beings, by offering your living
bodies as a holy sacrifice, truly pleasing
to God. Do not model yourselves on the
behavior of the world around you, but let
your behavior change, modeled by your new
mind. This is the only way to discover the
will of God, and know what is good, what it
is that God wants, what is the perfect thing
to do. (Rm 12:1, 2)

Motive for the performance of good acts—faith—is as important as the acts themselves:

Now it is impossible to please God
without faith, since anyone who comes to

him must believe that he exists and rewards
those who try to find him. (Heb 11:6)

Consequently, catechetical preaching, being founded on
the kerygma—the basic revelation of the saving act of
Jesus Christ—shows the believer how he can live out
the kerygma every day, in every action both as an individual person and also as a member of Christ's body.
United to Christ through faith, he lives thereby in a
community of fellow-believers, all of whom exercise in
a wonderful diversity the myriad gifts of the Holy Spirit.
It is not enough to be just and loving, generous and forgiving; these are only expressions of something deeper
and more profound—praise of God Himself. The Christian is above all one who gives thanks.

Content of Catechetical Preaching

The basic content of catechetical preaching in the
Roman Catholic Church is the sacraments and the moral
life of love. The life of human worship of the divine is
expressed not only through acts which are good in themselves, but it also receives through symbols a conscious,
cognitive expression as well. Each sacrament of the
Church symbolizes a particular aspect of human life
which has now been divinized by the specific intervention of God and the redeeming grace of Jesus Christ.
Catechetical preaching, therefore, gives the symbolic
worship of Christian faith, the sacraments, real meaning
to both the heart and mind of the worshipper so that the
symbol is itself productive of the grace it signifies. Catechesis makes the liturgical-sacramental act relevant to
the ordinary experience of life as it is lived daily—
through faith. For without faith, it is true to say there
are no sacraments.

One might have, for example, the real, sacramental presence of the Body and Blood, Soul and Divinity of Jesus Christ in the Eucharist through transubstantiation, but the Eucharist only becomes a sacramental symbol of saving power when it is received in faith—something neither a dog nor a pagan can do. In fact, anyone who receives the Eucharist without faith, that is "without recognizing the Body, is eating and drinking his own condemnation." (1 Cor 11:29)

The Sacraments

A good example of how catechetical preaching builds on the proclamation of the kerygma and channels it into the sacramental life of the believing community is the story of Philip's conversion of the Ethiopian eunuch and the eunuch's subsequent baptism. (Ac 8:26-40)

Philip was inspired by the Spirit and found himself running along side the Ethiopian's eunuch's chariot. As he ran alongside, he heard the eunuch reading aloud passages from Isaiah which foretold the suffering servant. When Philip asked the eunuch if he understood what he was reading, he replied that he could not understand unless somebody explained the meaning to him. Climbing into the chariot, Philip explained the Scriptures to the eunuch and showed that what he was reading was the prophecy of Jesus Christ, the suffering servant who would die for men's sins and free them from the bondage in which they were held enslaved.

Philip's kerygmatic proclamation burned itself into the Ethiopian eunuch's heart by the power of the Spirit so that his immediate desire was to become part of that saving mystery, to enter into the redemptive death of Christ in order that he might be free and live a new life in faith. When he asked what he must do to become one with Christ, Philip responded that he should be baptized. It was at that moment that they were passing by a pool of water, and so the eunuch went down into the water and Philip baptized him.

Paul explains:

> When we were baptized in Christ Jesus, we were baptized in His death. In other words, when we were baptized we went into the tomb with Him so that as Christ was raised from the dead by the Father's glory, we too might live a new life. If in union with Christ we have imitated His death, we shall also imitate Him in His resurrection. (Rm 6:3, 4)

When the eunuch came up from the water in which he had sacramentally died to sin, he arose a new creature, washed clean, refreshed, renewed. The Letter to the Ephesians continues the catechetical preaching on baptism when it not only exhorts all Christians to live out this baptismal life which begins in faith in a manner worthy of their calling, (Ep 4:1-7) but also reveals the nature of the unity into which the Christian has entered in Christ.

Like baptism, every other sacrament celebrates an aspect of living out the kerygma. While baptism celebrates death and rebirth, confirmation celebrates and bestows the strength of the Spirit. The Holy Eucharist is not only nourishment, but the whole liturgical rite of the Mass speaks of praise and thanksgiving because of our intimate communion with God and one another. Matrimony symbolizes and makes possible the life-long celebration of Jesus' revelation concerning the unity of Christ and the Church, and of husband and wife. Through sacred Christian marriage they form one indissoluble flesh so that their entire life together signifies the love Christ has for those who believe. All acts flowing from this holy bond, all the intimate family relations, all the love that is exchanged among family members, reflect the ceaseless activity of the Godhead known through faith. Husband and wife are living symbols of praise revealing to the Church that God is love.

The sacraments, therefore, flow from the kerygma and provide a means of expressing the saving truth in action as well as word. Through the sacraments, believers respond to the word they have accepted in faith, and their life-long sacramental response in the Spirit becomes itself a source of constant new strength. Catechesis is the kind of preaching which builds up faith so that the sacramental response has meaning and reflects accurately the inner life of the worshippers. It delivers the sacraments from any temptation to magic and superstition by nourishing the faith which gives them birth. Instead of a rite, they become a way of life.

A Biblical Mentality

Because the relation of kerygmatic proclamation to sacramental celebration is so intimate, it follows that fruitful catechetical preaching requires a profound biblical mentality on the part of the preacher. His teachings should not only flow from the Scriptures, they should lead back to a renewed understanding of the Scriptures, much like the experience of the early Church, which, as it grew in the mystery of Christ revealed by the apostles and celebrated in its communal life, was able to penetrate more completely into the meaning of the Old Testament.

Consequently, it is not enough simply to set up a series of questions and answers about the nature of God, man, and the Church, or to solve problems of ethics and morality. The answers may be of great significance to theologians and philosophers, but all too often the questions have never been asked by the listener, with the result that the answers—however valid—have no relevancy to his own needs, hurts or even his own experienced daily life of faith. Too often catechesis is equated with religious truths, when in fact it is as much a celebration of Christian mystery as is evangelization. Because the mystery of Christ is handed down to us in a normative form in Sacred Scripture, both evangelization and catechesis demand more than familiarity with selected epistles and gospels. They demand absolute immersion into the total Scripture. The greatest single problem with preaching today is that preachers are not immersed in Scripture. Other things are substitutes for it.

All scripture is inspired by God and can profitably be used for teaching, for refuting
error, for guiding people's lives and
teaching them to be holy. This is how
the man who is dedicated to God becomes
fully equipped and ready for any good work.
(2 Tm 3:16, 17)

On the other hand, catechetical preaching, particularly in these days of a tragically divided Christianity, will be developed in accord with varying Church traditions, since catechetical preaching inspires the new believer to live, not alone, but in a community of fellowbelievers, incorporating him into a full Church life and its communal worship. Catechesis teaches the re-born to meet the responsibilities of Christian fellowship and passes on the customs of his community for good order.
At the same time, of course, it forms him in a basic

Christian morality, conformed to the teachings of Christ, but always recognized as the fruit of the Spirit: "What the Spirit brings is very different: love, joy, peace, patience, kindness, goodness, trustfulness, gentleness and self-control." (Cf. Gal 5:13-26) Needless to say, the greatest fruit of the Spirit is the gift of love. (1 Cor 13)

Biblical catechesis, therefore, is principally ordered to the living of the sacraments of faith and outward expression of the life in Christ through the observance of Jesus' moral teachings. Through catechetical preaching the listener learns the meaning and the value of the signs by which the mystery of Christ is conveyed, in which it is contained, and through which it is manifested.

Modern Disaster Area

Because catechesis is a form of preaching, the characteristics common to all preaching need to be present if catechesis is to bear fruit in faith. Like all preaching, catechesis also requires personally experienced theological insight into the meaning of divine revelation, and as a result, the preacher-catechist must bear personal witness to his belief in the truth he proclaims. As Pope Paul VI said: "Modern man listens more willingly to witnesses than to teachers, and if he does listen to teachers, it is because they are witnesses." **(Evangelii Nuntiandi, No. 41)**

The reason so many religious education programs are failing today in parishes is because more time and energy are devoted to buying the right textbook series and designing curricula than to awakening the faith of the teachers. Yet, "religious education" teachers are, by virtue of their work, catechetical preachers receiving delegated "mission" from the pastor or bishop to touch the hearts and change the lives of their student-hearers. It is through preachers, not publishers' texts or film slides by themselves, that God has chosen to proclaim the good news.

Apathy

While at the present time most educational energy is being expended on the young, catechesis is actually more important for adults who are trying to live by faith in a complicated, demanding, pagan world where the influence of secularism is all pervasive. All too often, even the best-willed and most sincere person is compelled to live an adult life with the religious mind of a child, since the sad fact is that most Catholics, once they have completed the formal study of their religion, never study it again. Whether they stopped studying with First Holy Communion, age seven, or after Confirmation, age twelve, or even after graduation from a Catholic high school or college, published statistics reveal that 97% of Catholics, with few exceptions, never read a serious theological book, contemporary religious magazine, or Catholic newspaper (sales of which are counted in thousands). Above all, very few of the 48 million nominal Catholics read the Holy Bible seriously and consistently. The only source of their religious growth, therefore, is through attendance at Sunday Mass and listening to a Sunday sermon, yet today only about 50% of the Catholic population attends Mass on a regular weekly basis.

The lack of interest in further Christian education, the lack of desire to learn more about Jesus Christ, in short, religious apathy, is perhaps the greatest single indictment of an educational system which has for years been the greatest single formative influence in the life of the Catholic Christian. As so many Catholics testify, the education they received was basically a collection of catechism answers—truths about God—rather than the experience of fellow Christians bearing personal witness to the meaning of Jesus Christ as Lord and Saviour presented in a skillful and attractive way by persons who had reflected deeply on their gift of faith, and were able to articulate their experience of it so that others might enter into the Mystery of Christ with them.

Academics

Simply to survive, catechesis needs to be more than dry history of religion or the study of religious thought or the promulgation of a Christian idealism. Yet, in more and more Catholic educational institutes of all levels, including seminaries, comparative religion as a discipline is gaining status equal to theological reflection on and prayer-study of the Christian faith. Catechesis is a far more dignified and important ministry than academic study with its attendant danger of over-intellectualization which reduces the power of the Gospel to some kind of Christian philosophy of life.

Professionalism

A consequence of this trend towards the academic study of religion is the turning of religious education over to the so-called professional. Catholics probably have the most highly-trained cadre of professional religious educators the Church has ever enjoyed in its long history. Many enjoy prestigious titles, work with select committees, supervise large staffs, control respectable budgets and possess impressive academic credentials, and yet statistics show that in most places education is not a program, but a disaster area!

It is a disaster area because concern has centered on professional competence, knowledge and information,

and not on the faith revealed in the scripture and experienced in the catechist. Religious knowledge can be
passed on without faith, but faith cannot be passed on
without faith. Pope Paul VI asks: "In the long run, is
there any other way of handing on the gospel than by
transmitting to another person one's personal experience
of faith?" (Evangelii Nuntiandi, No. 46) Faith leads to
faith, or as scripture says: "the upright man finds life
through faith." (Rm 1:17)

After Evangelization

The necessity of faith is not limited to the catechist;
it is equally important that the one who is being catechized have already had the conversion experience con-
sequent upon the hearing of the evangelizing message.
The student listener must have undergone metanoia
and re-birth; he must profess in the depths of his heart
the Lordship of Jesus. Without this primary experience
of belief, even the most effective catechists preach to
deaf ears. Because this pre-requisite is not taken seriously for children—the eighth graders who have never
really been evangelized—there is the widespread phe-
nomenon of qualified and faith-filled religious educators
abandoning the classroom because they can no longer
face disinterested and unmotivated students who care
nothing for the experience of Jesus which the catechists
wish to share in faith.

The Thrust of Catechetics

A basic choice is made in the structuring of a catechetical preaching program when the preacher decides
either that catechesis is a search by man for the meaning
of life in Christ or the handing on of a revelation of God.

Obviously the two are closely connected, but it is a vastly different experience for the listener to hear one who is searching for meaning and to hear one who speaks confidently out of the Spirit which possesses him—the Power of God. The first is tentative, probing, exploratory; the second is certain, enriching and sure. Scripture itself encourages a view of catechesis which emphasizes the second approach when St. Peter writes: "By His divine power (Jesus) has given us all the things we need for life and for true devotion, bringing us to know God Himself, who has called us by His own glory and goodness." (2 P 1:3)

The mystery the catechist reveals through his preaching is inexhaustible, and as a result there will always be unanswered questions, since divine mystery has a way of raising more possibilities than the human mind can comprehend. Nevertheless, there is quite a difference between an abundance which leads to wonder and hunger for more, and an emptiness which compels desperate search. It may be necessary for modern man to get in closer touch with himself, and a variety of psychological techniques may be most helpful in this process; at the same time, it is questionable whether this search for inner meaning can replace the exposition of the Scriptures by preachers who have already entered into the mystery they proclaim through faith.

The Master Plan

It is precisely because of the magnitude of the task that faces the catechetical preacher to pass on the mystery of Christ through the symbols of the liturgy and the gifts of the Holy Spirit that have been revealed in the Sacred Scriptures, that catechesis requires a master plan which embraces all the aspects of the life of the Christian community at the parish level. Effective catechesis is possible when it follows a grand design that integrates liturgical celebration, including the contexts of the Sunday sermon, evangelization of the neighborhood, social action in matters of justice and charity, and all the other social, religious and economic programs that make up a vibrant parochial life.

It is counter-productive, for example, to teach in a religious education class the centrality of the Eucharistic liturgy when the celebration of the liturgy by the community is boring and uninspiring. It does not stimulate a faith experience to speak of the necessity of faith, if the parish does not have an active program of evangelization. It is not enough to plan single courses in scripture, history or ethics, if they are not integrated into a total experience of growing in the faith. A frequently mentioned reason for Catholic youth dropping out of religious education programs is that they experience endless repetition of the same old propositions and definitions, not growth in the mystery of Christ. In some cases, baptism has been taught to grade-schoolers, teen-agers and adult converts using the same words but in different books.

Without a master plan of total parish formation in the faith, everything becomes pretty much "catch-as-catch-can;" the problem today is that few are being caught.

Integral to the implementation of the master plan is that catechetical preaching always be connected to the reality of ordinary human existence and relevant, therefore, to daily life. Both young and old are turned off by the study of their religion when the truths they are learning seem remote from the realities they are experiencing, when demands exceed their capacities, when explanations are not helpful in enduring their sufferings. An effective test of whether or not the preacher is healing the hurts of his people is whether or not they are enthusiastic about listening to him, for enthusiasm, like humor, is only possible when it is real. In the context, therefore, of the real life experiences of those being catechized, the catechist, speaking to their felt-needs, seeks to unfold in an orderly and developed way the mystery of Christ and the ramifications of his salvation for a life of love and worship.

To put what has been said above into more colloquial terminology: the first question the catechist must answer in developing his master plan is "So What?" His words cannot heal if the hurt is not exposed; the heart will not be touched, if the mind is not excited; the mind will not be enlightened, if the insight does not interest. It is not enough, therefore, to develop a master plan on the basis of the orderly exposition of doctrine alone; the starting point of catechetical organization is the listener, because it is the listener's growth in faith for which the preacher is accountable.

Adult Formation

As was noted earlier, most catechetical energy is being exercised in the formation of children; however, there is growing evidence that the greatest problem in catechesis is not with the children, but with their parents and other adults. One incident illustrates the depth of the problem vividly.

A parish in the South had developed a rather innovative catechetical program, which had a rich scriptural foundation that led the children, (in this case teenagers), into a deep appreciation of its significance for their lives today. The catechetical team had spent many months preparing the program, and when the course was finally taught in the fall, it was enthusiastically received by the young people. One boy, about fifteen, was particularly excited by the course, and could not seem to get enough;

then, suddenly, he stopped coming. When the sister in charge of the program finally confronted the boy and pressed him regarding his dropping the course, she found out that when he would go home filled with enthusiasm about what he was learning and tried to share it with his parents, his father, in particular, would show disdain for "all this religion," and eventually the boy lost interest; the father's example was a far more powerful influence in real value-setting and life-motivation than any classroom instruction.

The anomaly is that while most religious education programs are still structured under the theory that learning takes place best in the classroom, more and more studies are indicating that the classroom is probably the one place where the least amount of life-learning goes on. Such studies reinforce the growing number of arguments that catechesis should take place outside the classroom in homes or other informal settings.

Some programs constructed along these latter lines are showing a significant success over more traditional methods of catechesis. Bible-sharing sessions, for example, are being held in the homes of parishioners where groups of young people and adults get together in an atmosphere of love to share their deepest thoughts on things most important to them. The young people have the opportunity of hearing people older than themselves and more experienced in the ways of Christ Jesus talking about him and the importance of His power for their lives. Such programs of Bible-sharing are by no means restricted to the young. The National Council of Catholic Women has instituted a national program to promote Bible-sharing among adult men and women of all ages, and similar programs are flourishing throughout the country.

An interesting and important sidelight on Bible-sharing is that it tends to be ecumenical, with Christians of different denominations finding a deep unity in the revealed Word of God.

It is clear from all that has been said, that catechesis cannot be limited to what has been traditionally understood as religious education, or even adult education. Its nature as a form of preaching demands the designing of an over-arching program which will create many exciting opportunities both inside and outside of school and classroom for the continual proclamation of God's word.

To implement such a program it will be necessary to utilize effective catechetical preachers. No one, for example, should attempt to catechize who has not had a personal experience of faith in Jesus Christ as Lord and Saviour; no one should be pressed into duty simply because a classroom needs a teacher; no one should be accepted for service simply because they have the academic qualifications. Insight into faith is fundamental to being a fruitful catechist.

In the same way, no one should be required to take or admitted into a catechetical offering at any age who has not acknowledged and experienced Jesus Christ as Lord and Saviour. It is fruitless to catechize a pagan.

Finally, all catechetical preaching and instruction—in liturgical settings, structured groupings or informal gatherings—springs from, is filled with and leads back to the Sacred Scriptures.

CHAPTER FOUR

DIDASCALIA

Highest Wisdom

The third, and most advanced, form of preaching is termed here **didascalia**. Like evangelization and catechesis, it, too, is a Greek derivative meaning highest wisdom or doctrine. Didascalia builds on evangelization and catechesis, carrying the experience of faith to its uttermost reaches of Christian possibility.

Presupposing that the listener has embraced Jesus Christ as Lord and Saviour and has been formed in the life of Christian worship, praise and thanksgiving, didascalia leads him to the fullest union with God the Father through Jesus Christ in the Holy Spirit. It proclaims both God's immanence and His transcendence, leading, thereby, to a full penetration into the mystery of Christ. Didascalia is the proclamation of the wisdom of the mature or perfect, the **teleoi** of which Paul speaks in 1 Corinthians 2:6-16. It is in the light of this "hidden wisdom of God which we teach in our mysteries" that Paul can ask the Philippians (3:8-16) to re-order their values and priorities so that the knowing of Christ and the sharing of His sufferings becomes the supreme goal of Christian living, because that is the way the Christian can hope to take his place in the resurrection of the dead. He concludes by noting: "We who are called 'perfect' must all think this way." (v. 15)

Hebrews (5:11-6:3) is another source for this understanding of the highest form of Christian preaching; here it presents the priesthood of Christ as advanced teaching, urging the reader: "Let us leave behind us then all the elementary teaching about Christ and concentrate on its completion without going over the fundamental doctrines again." (6:1) And it is of significance to note that those fundamental doctrines which are to be left behind are "the turning away from dead actions towards faith in God . . . the teaching about the resurrection of the dead, and eternal judgment." (6:2) These are seen as elementary teachings, milk for the immature, who are not yet capable of digesting solid food.

What is important for the mature Christian, the nourishment needed by one who is wise in the Lord, is to understand how, through the sacrifice of Christ—the Eternal High Priest—he has been delivered from sin. This is the substance of didascalic preaching which leads to the formation of the image of Christ in the believer. For, as Paul writes to the Corinthians, when the Christian contemplates Christ, as didascalic preaching leads him to do, he actually becomes the image he contemplates:

> We with our unveiled faces reflecting
> like mirrors, the brightness of the Lord,
> all glow brighter and brighter as we are
> turned into the image that we reflect; this
> is the work of the Lord who is Spirit. (2 Cor 3:18)

The Source of Wisdom

Because this highest wisdom flows from the **dynamis** of Christ, His ceaseless and inward power, it makes the mature Christian to be the light of the world and the salt of the earth. (Cf. Ph 2:13-16) Didascalia, wisdom, is a sharing of the very glory of God Himself—His **Doxa**—before which the angels stand in rapture.

It is not ourselves that we are preaching,
but Christ Jesus as the Lord, and ourselves as
your servants for Jesus' sake. It is the same
God that said, "Let there be light shining out
of the darkness," who has shone in our mind to
radiate the light of the knowledge of God's
glory, the glory on the face of Christ. (2 Cor 4:6)

Like Paul, the preacher, especially the didascalic preacher, is an ambassador of the mystery which has been revealed from above (Ep 3:1-11), and his task is to bind his hearers together in love and stir up their minds in faith so that they can penetrate the meaning of the mystery so fully that they really do know God's secret "in which all the jewels of wisdom and knowledge are hidden." (Col 2:2)

The Fruits of Wisdom

As the mature believer grows in the mystery, he finds that he is united not only to God, the source of wisdom, but also to his fellow believers. The knowledge the Spirit brings always leads to unity. Didascalia is not simply knowledge of abstract truth; it is wisdom which at the same time is power. In other words, in didascalic preaching, the preacher actually communicates God's power by which believers can sustain one another, even in persecution, and which enables them to lift up their voices in one united praise of God's glory. (Rm 15:1-6)

With Christian maturity the demands of discipleship are put into a reasonable context because now the Christian can judge all things by the light of Christ, since he already shares His glory. Consequently, the death to self which Jesus demands, the giving up of worldly possessions, the turning of the other cheek, the embracing of neighbor in constant love, which to the pagan are madness and unachievable, are experienced by the Christian as being most "reasonable" and possible because they bring us closest to God in both knowledge and love.

It is out of the abundance of this Christian wisdom which Paul was given through his gift of the Spirit that he could write to all Christians of all ages:

> I am certain of this: neither death nor life,
> no angel, no prince, nothing that exists,
> nothing still to come, not any power, or
> any height or depth, or any created thing can
> ever come between us and the love of God made
> visible in Christ Jesus our Lord. (Rm 8:38, 39)

Theological Insights of the Great

Roman Catholic preachers are blessed with a rich theological and mystical tradition upon which to draw for ever-fresh insights into the meaning of divine revelation which is particularly helpful when it comes to didascalic preaching. For example, there is St. Augustine's profound reflections on the Passion of Christ, St. Thomas's awe-inspiring, systematic treatment of the Trinity; there are the writings of the great mystics like St. Teresa of Avila on prayer or John Tauler on contemplation. Because these great Christians of the past wrote out of a profound experience of faith, their insights are as valid today as they were when they wrote them; yet, because they were written out of a different cultural milieu, they need translation into contemporary terms and culture. This is the work of the didascalic preacher. He takes the fruits of the great saints' understanding, and after having incorporated them into his own life of faith, shares them with his modern audiences, not as an academic exercise in the analysis of Christian thought, but as a vivid experience of God's presence and power in the Christian life today.

This is not as easy to do as it may at first seem. Perhaps it touches upon one of the greatest problems facing the preaching Church today. Preachers study theology and pass on its conclusions and sometimes even its processes of argumentation and the very language of the science itself, without first submitting it to the test of personally experienced faith.

Recently, a continuing education class of ordained priests was asked to name some great theologians; while the list they enumerated was extensive, five names were significantly absent: Matthew, Mark, Luke, John and Paul. Theology has come to mean simply an academic discipline or a philosophic inquiry into the nature of religious truth; it is scientific knowledge of God and man in relation to God. All too often, theology is taught in colleges, universities and even seminaries without any real reference to the experience of faith on the part of either teacher or student.

Before the didascalic preacher can insert divine meaning into the lives of his listeners, he must experience revelation as a vital part of his own life. To touch the hearts of others, he must speak out of the inward need to share his own enthusiastic appreciation of the Good News. If he does not need to say it, the listener does not need to hear it. If the truth he utters does not change his own life, he cannot expect it to change the lives of others. The evidence of many who have studied long hours of theology in the classroom is that theology has been so widely separated from faith experience that theological reflection is proving to be totally insufficient for effective didascalic preaching.

This point is illustrated by the following incident. In a homiletics class of ten seminarians, the first speaker gave an excellent exposition of the difference between transubstantiation and transignification. Since it was historically accurate and theologically nuanced, it was very well received by his classmates. Immediately after he concluded his talk, a second seminarian, who had been through the exact same theology course about the Eucharist, rose to give his talk. The second speaker paid tribute to his classmate's theological abilities and agreed wholeheartedly with his presentation; however, he had decided to speak on why one should go to Mass, even though it was such a dull and boring experience. Then he went on to say that as he was pondering the question, he realized he did not have any answer; therefore, he was throwing the question open to his classmates for their answers to the question, "Why go to Mass?" Not one member of this theologically astute class came up with a persuasive reason why a Christian should go to Mass!

It became evident in further discussion that although they knew theologically about the Eucharist, not one third year theologian present that day was able to articulate his own personal faith in the Real Presence of Jesus Christ in the sacrament. A few, in fact, admitted that they did not believe in the Real Presence, while the rest said they believed, but could not honestly put that experience of belief into words other than the theological formulae they had been taught. The significance of this isolated incident for the didascalic preacher is that it shows that in preaching he cannot be content with verbalizing theological arguments or proposing doctrinal conclusions no matter how well-founded. The preaching of the highest Christian wisdom can never be separated from personal reflection on daily faith experience—the mystery of Christ unfolding in the life of faith.

Social Action

The need for didascalic preaching today becomes apparent when it is realized that Christian social action flowing from faith, justice and love is an essential part of didascalia. Social action is basic to being a mature believer and a wise member of Christ's Body, since all Christian living is an expression of union with Jesus Christ and the result of living His life in the Spirit. Every act the believer performs is, through faith, an act of worship and praise; he does not love his neighbor or seek his welfare simply because of a reward that will be given sometime in the future. Love of neighbor is possible and necessary now because Jesus loves those whom He has chosen and His love is always active within them. It is this understanding of love as the cause, not the reward, of good actions that permeates the First Letter of John:

> We are to love, then,
> because he loved us first.
> Anyone who says, "I love God,"
> and hates his brother
> is a liar,
> since a man who does not love the brother he can see
> cannot love God, whom he has never seen.
> (1 Jn 4:19)

Social action, therefore, is the inevitable fruit of believing in Jesus, and social concern becomes more urgent as the believer enters more fully into the mystery revealed. Sometimes social action is unfortunately taught as part of catechetics, and while this is valid to some extent, only adequate formation in the full mystery of Christ can provide sufficient motivation for persevering in activities which very often are more divisive and disruptive than unifying and comforting. Just as visions sustained the prophets of old, so too the vision revealed by wisdom preaching best sustains the Christian social actionist in the face of misunderstanding, rejection and persecution.

How the possession of Christian wisdom modifies one's perception of the world is illustrated in terms of reaction to the evil that he perceives. There is no cause for the believing Christian to be shocked at the vicious animal behavior of the pagan: violence, crime, sex, greed, murder are a way of life to him who has been so wounded by sin. The only reason the Christian does not commit these crimes against God and man is the healing grace of God saving him from the power of sin and giving him the power to act from love. Indignation, shock and rage at abortion, for example, are inappropriate responses from one who is holy only because he has received the mercy of God delivering him from a life of evil. Sorrow for the suffering that sin causes, compassion for the sinner and a desire to better the world through the proclamation of the Gospel are more reflective of an understanding of the divine dynamic which is at work in the world, transforming it and bringing it into perfect submission to and union with Christ. The motive Scripture gives believers for having complete confidence in Christ when they are in need of help is that he understands human weakness and temptations. (Cf. Heb 4:15)

Knowing God

The search for God has characterized human life in all cultures. No thinking person can gaze at the immense complexity of our universe without wondering about the Force that designed it and keeps it in being. Chance and random motion do not satisfy the perceptive mind;

clearly there must be Something behind the order—a Purpose, and a Power. Throughout history this search has taken many forms; from the simplest to the most complicated, from the bizarre to the mundane. For Christians, the long search is over.

The ultimate gift that is given to Christian believers is authentic knowledge about the Being who has created all. The knowledge that is given in Jesus Christ is not simply the satisfaction of a natural and healthy curiosity; it is a knowledge which brings men and women into union with God and one another since the life of Jesus is the revelation of His glory, a glory which is reflected always in the lives of those who possess the truth of faith. As the believers put on the mind of Christ and become like Him, even to bearing His wounds in their flesh through suffering, Christians become one with the Power Who is now revealed as the Loving Father.

Jesus Christ has come into the world to give light to their lives so that Christians no longer stumble about in the darkness of sin and despair. The Christian does not struggle with the basic questions of life: Who am I? Where am I going? Why was I born? How can I be happy and fulfilling? How can I get the most out of life? He has the answers to these questions in Christ; answers which are not just abstract guidelines, directives and laws. His answers are experienced in terms of specific thrusts, desires, abilities, circumstances and events. He recognizes that he is being guided from above, kept safe from harm and led into new, exciting directions of creative love. In this light, the most routine job or dull undertaking becomes personally fulfilling because it is done in obedience to the will of the Father. Among the early Christians, even slaves could find fulfillment by uniting themselves to Christ, and so can modern man pressured though he is by the demands of contemporary society.

Today's Christian is able to test the authenticity of his answers through the Spirit that is given to him, a Spirit which is so powerfully present in his life that it seems heaven has already begun on earth. As a result, the Christian is not afraid of death or future judgment. On the contrary, he lifts up his eyes and waits for the future with happy anticipation, because his life of love now gives him the perfect assurance in Christ Jesus that he will not be condemned. Judgment is being exercised now in the Spirit. Those who reject Jesus condemn themselves, but those who call upon His Name, put on His mind and live in His light already experience the life of the world to come through faith and in peace and joy.

Thus, the Second Coming of Christ is already being given its present experience in the Spirit. While the Christian eyes the future with hope of even greater and richer fulfillment, especially through the resurrection of the Body, he does not look for the literal translation into reality of the apocalyptic images of the end-times. Through faith and the experience of the Spirit, the Second Coming of Christ is already present to him. He has already been reborn into the eternal order, evil has already been definitively overcome by the Cross, and the reign of God is already marvelously at work. God has been revealed in Jesus Christ and with that revelation the purpose of creation has been achieved, although not yet completed.

Furthermore, it is through the experience of the presence of Christ in the Spirit that the Christian is able to understand the mysterious events of Christ's suffering and death; only the resurrection and the out-pouring of the Holy Spirit can explain the Passion and the Cross. The process of Christian understanding is reflected in the Gospel of John, written, as exegetes are able to account for through a complex process, some sixty years after the Resurrection of Jesus.

When John preached, and his preaching was recorded for posterity, John spoke of a man he knew. He wrote, not just about a man he knew and who had lived in the past when John was a teenager, about someone he was familiar with only as living on earth in the flesh. The man Jesus, of whom he wrote, was also the God who was present to him throughout his long lifetime—in the Spirit. Jesus was as present to John through faith as He is to every Christian living today. In fact, Jesus was more present to John after His resurrection than He could possibly have been before His death when still in the flesh and subject to its restrictions of physical presence, time and space.

Therefore, in writing his Gospel, John looked back on the events of Jesus' life and discerned a pattern he had not been aware of before. He recalls the events, not just in their historical, geographical order and relevance, but theologically as they unfold the true nature, person and mission of Jesus, the Christ, the Messiah, the Saviour, the Son of God.

A particularly apt example of this reflective process occurs in the composition of Jesus' discourse on Himself as the Bread of Life in John 6:22-59. Here the gospel writer has taken the gist of Jesus' teachings given on many occasions and artfully combined them in a single dramatic incident. Such a theologically revealing discourse is the work of The Spirit who enables the writer to judge the particular occasions when Jesus spoke on the Bread of Life in the light of His over-arching mission. John perceived a pattern of revelation which was far more significant than the isolated incidents. In revealing the pattern John enables the reader to recognize the

Eucharist celebrated by his community for what it is: The Body and Blood of Christ.

John's gospel is the revelation of the glory of God Himself, the glory possessed by Jesus and given to those who have faith; to know Jesus is to know God Himself, and that knowledge is eternal life. No matter how frail, unworthy, transitory his nature, through faith in Jesus and filled with his Spirit as a member of His body, each Christian even today is able to converse with God anytime he wants as God's child and His close friend.

When St. Paul reflects on the gift that has been given to the Christian, he is filled with awe and driven to praise God:

> Glory to him who is able to give you the
> strength to live according to the Good News
> I preach, and in which I proclaim Jesus Christ,
> the revelation of the mystery kept secret
> for endless ages, but now so clear that it
> must be broadcast to pagans everywhere to
> bring them to the obedience of faith. This
> is only what Scripture has predicted, and it
> is part of the way the eternal God wants things
> to be. He alone is wisdom; give glory to Him
> through Jesus Christ, for ever and ever amen.
> (Rm 16:25-27)

CHAPTER FIVE

THE LITURGICAL HOMILY

Function-Indicating, not Content-Determining

A great deal of confusion revolves around the nature of the liturgical homily because the term "homily" has been given so many different interpretations. Unfortunately, the documents of the Second Vatican Council, which first popularized the term in recent times, are not helpful in arriving at a refined sense since they use the terms homily, sermon, admonition, instruction, **institutio** interchangeably, without definable differences. However, a common understanding of the Eucharistic "homily" that seems to be operative in preaching is that it is a commentary on, or explanation of, the scripture readings of the Mass of the day. According to this understanding, the thing that distinguishes the homily from other forms of preaching is its scriptural content.

As a result, almost all preaching at Mass follows an invariable formula of taking the scripture readings, trying to determine a central theme common to them all, explaining something of the exegesis of the texts, what the original situation was and what it means for the Christian of today, and making a practical application of this to everyday life, usually in terms of moral living. Already, the problems connected with this limited notion of homily are beginning to surface.

For one thing, it is a very repetitive and monotonous form of preaching which will become even more so as the reading cycles are repeated. Most of the reading selections are brief, their teachings limited, and in many cases, especially with the gospels, the text is clear itself, (which is why it was written to begin with).

For example, the pericope about Peter's walking on the water, becoming frightened, calling out to Jesus and being saved is obvious; consequently, the preacher who limits himself to a restricted understanding of "homily" is forced into some rather far-fetched accomodations at times just for variety's sake.

On the other hand, large areas of traditional Catholic doctrine are never examined because the Scripture texts which specifically refer to them are not read on Sundays; for example, James' letter, which forms the basis for the Church's understanding of the anointing of the sick.

What is being suggested here is that the thing that distinguishes the homily as a form of preaching is not its scriptural content since it is the clear teaching of the Church that all preaching is to be scriptural—flowing from Scripture and leading to a deeper appreciation of Scripture. What characterizes the homily is the function it serves in the Christian liturgy. "Homily" is not a content-determining word, but a function-indicating one.

Homily: Arousal to Worship

The homily is a short sermon integrally related to a liturgical act which inspires the worshipper to participate in the liturgy more fully in faith. A baptismal homily reveals to the Christian community and the one being baptized, the relationship of his new act of faith to his entrance into the Christian community and the mystery of Christ; the Eucharistic homily manifests how the Mass participants are joined in perfect praise with the Sacrifice of Calvary in Jesus. The wedding homily increases the power of the sacrament in the lives of the married couple by relating the wedding ceremony to Jesus' love for His Church and the couple's love for one another as Christian witness to the world.

In other words, the liturgical homily manifests the present significance of the liturgical act in such a way as to incorporate the worshippers more fully in the act of worship by arousing their faith and the dispositions of that faith appropriate to the liturgical act, so that the effects of the sacrament extend beyond the immediate sacramental celebration into all phases of their daily life and the life of the entire Church.

To do this, of course, the homilist necessarily uses Sacred Scripture. Indeed, the Church teaches that Sacred Scripture and appropriate liturgical texts should be the main source for the homily. They are used because, when they are expressed by preachers of faith, the Word of God has the ability to rouse the listeners to acts of deeper belief in the presence, power and love of God. Using mainly Scripture and speaking from his faith, the preacher is able in the Spirit to stir people up to greater trust in God's saving intervention in their lives, especially by encouraging them to greater confidence in the Spirit which has been given to them.

This enables the worshippers to accept more readily and joyfully God's designs for their sanctification, their lives and their service. It enables them to discern more perfectly the will of God which is manifested to them not only through Sacred Scripture, the teaching of Christ's Church, but also through the events of their lives, day by day.

Paul sums up what the homilist does when he writes:

Think of God's mercy, my brothers, and worship him, I beg you, in a way that is worthy of thinking beings, by offering your living bodies as a holy sacrifice, truly pleasing to God. Do not model yourselves on the behavior of the world around you, but let your behavior change, modeled by your new mind. This is the only way to discover the will of God and know what is good, what it is that God wants, what is the perfect thing to do. (Rm 12:1, 2)

From this, it is clear that the homily does not so much explain the scriptural texts, as by using Scripture, it explains how the liturgical act which is being celebrated connects with the reality of everyday Christian living.

It is from the scriptures that the actions and signs [of the liturgy] derive their meaning. Thus to achieve the restoration, progress, and adaptation of the Sacred liturgy, it is essential to promote that warm and living love for scripture to which the venerable tradition of both eastern and western rites gives testimony. **(Constitution on the Sacred Liturgy, No. 24)**

The homily reveals the liturgy and shows how Christ is touching the worshipper through the sacrament which is now being celebrated in faith. As an example, consider the most common liturgical celebration, the Eucharist: The Eucharist is basically a thanksgiving service, praising God through Jesus Christ, for the great gifts He has given His brothers and sisters. All the prayers, prefaces, canons are redolent with this. Consequently, it follows that the basic purpose of the Eucharistic homily is not to explain the lectionary cycle, but to awaken anew for each Eucharistic celebration the sentiments of praise, worship and thanksgiving, which is done by Christians calling to mind Jesus' death, resurrection and ascension into glory. Furthermore, in the liturgical celebration not only is mystery revealed through symbols and saving events recreated, but the very power of God touches and transforms those who give praise.

In the Eucharist, while His People offer praise to God,

He, more importantly, gives Himself to them again and again in word and sacrament so that they are lifted out of their precarious existence bordering on calamity into a new life which is His Own, and which is the pledge of eternal happiness and divine fulfillment. Although the believer's participation in such a mysterious yet powerful action starts with scriptural revelation, the depth of the mystery cannot be fathomed simply through historical analysis and exegetical considerations of selected pericopes; neither can it be explored through gospel paraphrases. The words and actions which symbolize what God is doing now touch only the outer limits of a profound act whose vast dimensions can only be glimpsed by men and women of faith.

However dissatisfied some might be with current liturgical practices, the fact remains that the sacramental liturgy is the vital physical link with the glorified Christ, and the homilist devotes his spiritual energies, theological insights and creative talents to making the implications of that fact somewhat realized in the lives of the worshippers. It is this physical linkage that makes the mystery encountered in the liturgy real and the celebration relevant to the lives of those who have gathered in faith.

Consequently, the problem with the homily is not a problem of a central theme, effective format, scriptural exegesis and practical application. The real problem of the homily is the preacher's own participation in the mystery of the liturgical celebration as a deep experience of his faith in Jesus Christ as Lord and Saviour.

The Creative Effort

No matter how much one may theologize about the nature and purpose of the liturgical homily, ultimately the homily has to be prepared, and frequently the lack of adequate preparation is the cause of poor homilies. To illustrate the importance of adequate preparation for effective speaking, most speech composition books distinguish the different kinds of speeches on the basis of the amount and kind of preparation that goes into them.

First, there is the impromptu speech which requires little or no preparation. It is the kind of informal discourse that springs into being when one is suddenly called upon for a few remarks, and rapidly tries to put together a few thoughts in some kind of reasonable order. The delightful thing about the impromptu speech is that, being so spontaneous, the speaker's natural wit and personality is able to shine through effortlessly. When impromptu speeches are brief, they are usually enjoyable, especially if the speaker has any natural flair for expressing himself.

The difficulty with the impromptu speech, however, is that it depends solely on the habitual knowledge of the speaker since he does not have a chance to research his subject; it also tends to ramble, since there has not been enough time to organize thoughts effectively. Such superficial thinking and rambling is not particularly noticeable in a short speech on a light subject, but if it is extended for any length of time on subject of some consequence, by a person not especially gifted, the result is banality and boredom. Most after dinner speakers become adept at impromptu speaking, and can be entertaining and winning with little preparation.

A second kind of speech, the manuscript speech, is at the opposite end of the spectrum from the impromptu. It is the result of extensive preparation through research and study, with much attention being given to structure and phrasing so that the finished product is perceptive and persuasive. Political speakers, among others, employ teams of writers to prepare just the right speech for various occasions, hoping that carefully worked out, ringing phrases will become part of the common folk expression. "Ask not what your country can do for you; ask what you can do for your country" (John F. Kennedy's famous slogan).

Unfortunately, because the manuscript speech undergoes such careful word by word scrutiny, it has a tendency to become stilted; the manner of expression takes on undue importance so that even substance is sacrificed for the felicitous phrase. In delivery, it is frequently poorly read, resulting in a monotonous and indirect communication. Because speeches which are read are usually difficult to absorb, published manuscripts can be very helpful to the audience by permitting them, at their leisure, to reflect on what was said. On the other hand, if the speech is well-done, it can constitute a great moment in the communication of insight and experience, precisely because of the amount of thought that has gone into its preparation.

From all points of view, the most effective speech is the extemporaneous speech, combining the strengths of both the manuscript speech and the impromptu. The extemporaneous speech is as carefully and fully prepared as the manuscript speech; indeed, in its original form it may be a manuscript speech; however, before delivery, the manuscript is put aside except for particularly effective or important passages, and a tight outline is made of the entire speech which serves as a guide to the speaker who simply talks his ideas in the language that comes most naturally to him. Thus, the extemporaneous speech goes beyond superficial thinking and habitual knowledge. It is carefully structured for maximum intellectual and emotional effect, yet it allows the element of informality and spontaneity to express itself in language with which the speaker is most at home, avoiding thereby a literary stiltedness.

Extemporaneous speaking, of course, is the most difficult to do well and consumes the greatest amount of time because the creative act which is required for both the inspiration and execution of the inspiration is not under the direct control of the will; it cannot be commanded on a time schedule. Insight must be wooed in an atmosphere free of constraint, and good organization and succinct phrasing are the fruit of many hours of reflection and re-writing. Yet, an incisive speech is worth the effort.

In the practical order, however, it is the experience of many Church-goers that, with rare exceptions, the Sunday homily is only an impromptu speech, with all its accompanying weaknesses. Consequently, perhaps the first step in a preacher's efforts to renew his preaching is to adopt the extemporaneous speech form as the usual form of gospel preaching.

So What?

The greatest and most significant idea in the world can be irrelevant to an audience unless it bears upon their life situation. The emergency care of a dialysis patient, for example, is really only of concern to those responsible for caring for such persons, even though the subject of itself is intensely interesting, and under certain conditions, essential for human life. Hearing a talk on the subject, however, is not likely to excite most audiences, simply because they have no need for that information, and although a doctor's enthusiasm for the subject may engender a sympathetic ear for awhile, ultimately, unless he can connect it to the felt needs of his audience, it is not likely to have wide appeal.

Statistics tell us that Christian teachings are also perceived as irrelevant to the real needs of life by many. The preacher may be convinced of their importance, but unless he can convince his audience of the value of the

Good News for their personal lives, the lives of their families, and for society as a whole, the Church will not be able to extend its influence significantly.

Therefore, the most important question the preacher has to answer each time he speaks is "So What?" He needs to gain the interest of his audience and convince them that what he is saying is of such significance to them that they should listen to him speak on the subject he has chosen. Such an approach seems obvious when boldly stated; yet, most sermons do not use the felt need of the audience as the basic principle of homily organization. Instead they begin with the text of the day, or the theological point to be made, or the liturgical event being celebrated, but not the hurt of the hearer. However, God's word is a healing word that is meant to heal the wounded heart and the sinful life, so if the hurt is not recognized and the wound is not acknowledged, the healing cannot take place. It does little good to instruct an audience in what it should do with regard to salvation, if the audience does not recognize its need for it.

An incident illustrative of the consequences of failing to answer "So What?" occurred when a visitor attended a Mass in which the preacher started his homily by remarking: "We are filled with joy today as we celebrate the feast of St. Francis." The visitor being totally unaware that it was the feast of St. Francis, and consequently not in the frame of mind attributed to him by the preacher, dismissed the entire sermon in that one sentence as irrelevant and did not bother to listen further.

An Approach

Because the experience and insights to be conveyed in a sermon vary so widely, the personalities of the preachers are so diverse, and the needs of the audiences so different, it is impossible to give a fixed format for any kind of sermon, especially for one that is as demanding as the homily. On the other hand, there is an approach that can be used in the creation of a sermon that assists the preacher in organizing his materials in a way that will attract and hold the attention and interest of his audience: The Hurt-Healing Approach.

In this approach, the preacher begins by identifying in some way the hurt in the lives of his audience: loneliness, frustration, self-hatred, anger, sickness, fear. After having developed the possible manifestations of this hurt in one's relations to God and fellow human beings, the preacher then shows how the Word of God, divine revelation, addresses itself in power to hurt, especially the wound of sin, in a way which is healing. The substance of the sermon, therefore, is a developed insight into how God's power is operative in the lives of everyone, bringing them into closer union with Himself through Jesus Christ in faith.

For example, St. Thomas Aquinas notes that most sins are committed because of fear, the fear of rejection by God or man. Thus, humans acquire money with a passion in order to experience security for the present and the future. This can become greed which eventually drives out any concern for others, stifles love and reduces the miserly person to pathetic isolation and alienation. The resulting loneliness has driven people to suicide; yet the reason for their loneliness is that fear has dried up love within them, and they are unable to extend themselves to others.

God's Word heals the killing wound of fear by revealing His endless love. He will never reject His chosen ones because of His son Jesus, who died on the Cross that His brothers and sisters might live. His death gives the believer the perfect motive for confident hope. (Rm 5:9-11)

The ramifications of this revelation for Christian living are inexhaustible. and the revelation of this love is itself a power which can change lives and heal the wounds of fear, greed and loneliness.

Conclusion

There is no more exciting ministry given to mankind than the ministry of preaching. To be a proclaimer of God's Word is to be the messenger of His salvation. The preacher's growth in the Word teaches him his own dependence on God for everything in his life, and this dependence in turn opens him to the fullest experience of the divine power. It is true to say that the preacher speaks not only to his audience, but to himself; when he utters God's word in faith, he not only is preacher, he is also hearer, so that in the very act of preaching, the preacher brings to himself as well as to others the Gospel Power which is Eternal Life.

APPENDIX A

THANK GOD! HE LOVES ME!

Religion: A Joy, Not A Burden

Most sermons today say only one thing: "Try Harder!" **Try Harder** sermons are at the core of the decline of Christianity because they do not hold out hope to people struggling with life, only endless challenge to do more. **Try Harder** preaching does not proclaim the Good News, it just passes out good advice. It does not proclaim the Lordship of Jesus, only the responsibilities of man. It is not concerned with God's initiative in saving man from sin, but with man's response—not what God does for us, but what we must do for God. So many people have told me that all they hear from the pulpit is: "By good deeds we earn eternal life." Moralizing has replaced the Gospel in Sunday sermons, and the avoidance of sin is given more importance than the experiencing of God's love.

Once I was trapped in the middle of a family fight that had evidently been raging for months. When the teen-age daughter objected for the hundredth time to going to Mass on Sunday because she "didn't get anything out of it," her father, a staunch Catholic, finally yelled at her in exasperation: "Look, no one wants to go to Mass. You don't want to go to Mass. Your mother doesn't want to go to Mass. I don't want to go to Mass. But as long as you are living under my roof and eating my food, you are going to Mass whether you like it or not, and I don't want to hear another word about it!"

Clearly, neither father nor daughter expected anything more out of going to Mass than the fulfillment of an unplesant duty. The father was willing to endure because he was sure he would be rewarded sometime in the future. The daughter was not, so she wanted out.

I discovered later that for both father and daughter all of religion was like the Mass, something tediously demanding. Fear made the father religious; boredom drove the daughter away. Neither heard Jesus say:

> Come to me all you who labor and are burdened, and I will give you rest. Shoulder my yoke and learn from me for I am gentle and humble in heart and you will find rest for your souls. Yes, my yoke is easy and my burden light. (Mt 11:28-30)

The truth of the matter is that believing in Jesus makes life easier to live, not harder. When we trust in Jesus, all things are transformed: suffering brings strength, poverty is enriching, terrors are laid to rest by love, and life gains meaning and purpose. In short, the believer experiences for himself that Jesus does bestow a more abundant, full and rewarding life, as He promises: "I have come so that they may have life and have it to the full" (Jn 10:10).

So, if religion makes us feel inadequate, it may be because we have unwittingly fallen into an old heresy with a fancy name: **semi-Pelagianism.** By denying that salvation is a totally free gift of God in both its beginnings and its ultimate effects, semi-Pelagianism places the burden of eternal happiness on our weak wills and our uncertain constancy rather than on the unchanging foundation of God's unending love. Jesus says: "No one can come to me unless he is drawn by the Father who sent me, and I will raise him up on the last day." (Jn 6:44).

First preached in the 5th century, semi-Pelagianism has gained widespread, if unrecognized, acceptance in our own time. Yet, it did not heal hurting hearts then, and it is not healing them today. However, every heresy, even semi-Pelagianism, has some truth to it, so that when we try to separate the truth from the error in a mystery as profound as "predestination," or how God loves us, it is necessary to approach the whole matter patiently, with a prayer-filled heart and the willingness to do a mental stretch.

The purpose of this writing is to encourage believing Christians to have complete confidence in God's power to rescue us from our sins and make us holy, loving and happy. Jesus tells us:

> Yes, God loved the world so much
> that he gave his only Son,
> so that everyone who believes in him may not be lost
> but may have eternal life.
> For God sent His Son into the world
> not to condemn the world,
> but so that through him the world might be saved.
> No one who believes in him will be condemned;
> but whoever refuses to believe is condemned already,
> because he has refused to believe
> in the name of God's only Son. (Jn 3:16-18)

Our lives as Christians in this world are the fruit of God's love. Each day, we who believe in Jesus, are transformed by His love so that in God's time and in God's way we become the images of His Son, Jesus, which He has willed to us to be from all eternity. Since His love in our hearts is the sure sign of God's presence, and since the other gifts of the Spirit are the effects of His saving activity within us, we who believe can rest secure in the knowledge that through faith in Jesus Christ, we are being delivered from sin and prepared for an eternal life of happiness. St. Paul assures us:

> With God on our side who can be against us? Since God did not spare his own Son, but gave him up to benefit us all, we may be certain, after such a gift, that he will not refuse anything he can give. Could anyone accuse those that God has chosen? When God acquits, could anyone condemn? Could Christ Jesus? No! He not only died for us—he rose from the dead, and there at the right hand stands and pleads for us.
>
> Nothing therefore can come between us and the love of Christ, even if we are troubled or worried, or being persecuted, or lacking food or clothes, or being threatened or even attacked. As scripture promised: **For your sake we are being massacred daily, and reckoned as sheep for the slaughter.** These are the trials through which we triumph, by the power of him who loved us.
>
> For I am certain of this: neither death nor life, no angel, no prince, nothing that exists, nothing still to come, not any power, or height or depth, nor any created thing can ever come between us and the love of God made visible in Christ Jesus our Lord. (Rm 8:31-39)

No wonder each one of us can say with genuine joy: "Thank God! He loves me!"

The Merit System—An American Dream

Semi-Pelagianism

According to semi-Pelagianism:

All men are spiritual equals. No one has been specially chosen and set apart in contrast to anyone else. No one has been given any more than anybody else. There is no body of the elect, pre-destined from all eternity. Rather, God has called all men to salvation without respect of persons, and He has given to each one sufficient grace to enter into eternal life. However, in order for this grace to actually achieve the end for which it was given to all, it is necessary that a man or woman use it properly. In other words, because man is free, he must respond to that grace and use it in a way which pleases God so that God will be moved to reward him with eternal life. Salvation therefore, is not simply something God gives, it is something that we must earn by the quality of the lives we lead.

If we fail, therefore, to use the grace God pours out upon us in sufficient manner to bring us to heaven, then we cannot expect God to save us. If we do not keep working at our spiritual life day after day, we cannot expect God to help us. After all, according to this heresy, God helps only those who help themselves. While prayer is important, works are more so, "So pray as if everything depends on God, but work as if everything depends on you." If one lives his whole life in this way, then God will have to reward him. So we can take consolation in the fact that no matter how much we suffer, or how hard we work, if we hang in there, gritting our teeth, persevering in good works until the end, we will be rewarded for our efforts.

Those people, therefore, who do not keep the law, who neglect their spiritual lives and religious practices, and simply trust that God will get them through are the most deceived of all. That is why it is so important to stress the keeping of the commandments and the religious practices by which one daily grows in the imitation of Christ. For He is our model; in imitating His virtues, especially His patient endurance of suffering by carrying our own daily cross, we will merit a life of eternal happiness with Him in heaven.

Life on earth may be very hard because it is a testing period; yet, happiness will come to those who pass their trials. God will reward those who have proven their faithfulness. That is why sin is such a tragedy; it cuts us off from God, and God will not be able to help us bcause we have abused and misused the grace He has already given us. In giving us the commandments and the example of Christ, God has shown us the way, and if we do not follow the way, then we can hardly expect God to give us what we obviously do not really want, treasure or value. Our perverse will, therefore, can frustrate even the most generous intentions of God.

So much for semi-Pelagianism. I imagine by this time most readers will be saying to themselves, "What's wrong with that? That is what I was taught. That is what Catholicism says." In other words, many do not even see heresy in the above. Yet, **semi-Pelagianism** is just a watered-down form of **Pelagianism,** another even more ancient and dangerous heresy, which is also very popular today and is the theological counterpart of modern theories of education that are forming American society.

Pelagianism

Pelagianism teaches that man, untouched by original sin, is basically good willed and that it is only necessary to point out the directions his life should take for him to be a happy, productive person. If a person knows what is right, he will do it. Consequently, God sent Christ to give us the living example of the good life; He points the way to us so that we will not be deceived by the vain transitory delights of this world, but rather through death to self, and living for others, we will receive the reward of eternal life.

Omitting reference to eternal life, modern educational theories say basically the same thing. They teach that if we can only overcome unfavorable environmental influences and provide the right kind of education adapted to the needs and talents of the child, the child will respond in a positive manner and become a good citizen. Hence, it is necessary that parents send their children to school to learn not merely the skills by which they can acquire more knowledge and express themselves, but also in order that they might learn how to relate to others as part of the productive American society.

Indeed, as we extend equal opportunity to all members of society, women and minorities, each will be able to achieve the good life. Our folklore abounds with examples of the self-made man who was able to overcome obstacles and achieve success. It may be more difficult now, with the complexities that an expanding population gives us; nevertheless, as long as we keep trying to free ourselves from the encumbrances of disease, poverty and repression, each will be able to attain the goal he sets for himself. It is the American dream, and it is being realized every day.

Well, if the above is heresy, just what does the Gospel of Jesus Christ reveal?

The Divine Plan

God is Supreme

Scripture tells us that because He is an intelligent being, God has a plan. The all-powerful Creator of the entire world and everything in it has created a master design to reflect His glory and His power and His love. However, we human beings have trouble grasping God's plan because it is so far beyond our wildest dreams or imaginings. We live in a world of constant limitation; every day we see countless manifestations of weakness and sometimes malice: war, poverty, exploitation, sensuality, stupidity and alienation. Consequently, it is difficult for us to see beyond human failure to even faintly conceive of the absolute power, wisdom and goodness of God.

Yet, this absolute goodness is the basis for all that happens in the world and to us, and unless we appreciate the greatness of the One by Whom we have been created, we can never fully appreciate the greatness of the Love that gave us life.

All that happens in the world must necessarily happen because of the Divine Love. Nothing can escape the notice or power of God. He is All, and not even man's freedom can possibly frustrate or change God's overarching will.

I am God unrivalled
God who has no like.
From the beginning I foretold the future,
and predicted beforehand what is to be.
I say: My purpose shall last;
I will do whatever I choose.
I call a bird of prey from the east,
my man of destiny from a far country.

No sooner is it said than done,
no sooner planned than performed. (Is 46:10-11)

At the same time, both our experience of life and the revelation of Sacred Scripture make it clear that man is truly free:

(God) Himself made man in the beginning,
    and then left him free to make his own decisions.
If you wish, you can keep the commandments,
    to behave faithfully is within your power.
He has set fire and water before you;
    put out your hand to whichever you prefer.
Man has life and death before him;
    whichever a man likes better will be given him.
For vast is the wisdom of the Lord;
    He is almighty and all-seeing.
His eyes are on those who fear Him,
    He notes every action of man.
He never commanded anyone to be godless
He has given no permission to sin. (Si 15:14-21)

Reconciliation in Jesus

These two seemingly opposite, contradictory truths—that man has free will, but that God's will prevails wherever good is done—lie at the heart of understanding the way of God with man. They must be reconciled, brought together into a single vision of reality, a perspective which permits us to see and to experience the dignity and wonder of the Creator/Father and His creatures/children—men and women, you and me.

That fusion of divine power and human freedom is brought about in Jesus Christ through love. God is Love. He created a world of beauty and order to share His own fullness of life—His very being—with those He has called

into existence. The apex of this creative design of love
is a man—Jesus Christ. To the Christians at Ephesus, a
writer inspired by God Himself summarizes in moving
language and vivid images the greatness and scope of
the Divine Plan of Salvation.

> Blessed be God the Father of our Lord Jesus Christ,
> who has blessed us with all the spiritual blessings of
>   heaven in Christ.
> Before the world was made, he chose us, chose us in
>   Christ,
> to be holy and spotless, and to live through love in
>   his presence,
> determining that we should become his adopted sons,
>   through Jesus Christ
> for his own kind purposes,
> to make us praise the glory of his grace,
> his free gift to us in the Beloved,
> in whom, through his blood, we gain our freedom,
>   the forgiveness of our sins.
> Such is the richness of the grace
> which he has showered on us
> in all wisdom and insight.
> He has let us know the mystery of his purpose,
> the hidden plan he so kindly made in Christ from
>   the beginning
> to act upon when the times had run their course to
>   the end:
> that he would bring everything together under
>   Christ, as head,
> everything in the heavens and everything on earth.
> And it is in him that we were claimed as God's own,
> chosen from the beginning,
> under the predetermined plan of the one who guides
>   all things
> as he decides by his own will;

chosen to be,
for His greater glory,
the people who would put their hopes in Christ
    before he came.
Now you too, in him,
have heard the message of the truth and the good
    news of your salvation
and have believed it;
and you too have been stamped with the seal of the
    Holy Spirit of the Promise
the pledge of our inheritance
which brings freedom for those whom God has taken
    for His own,
to make His glory praised. (Ep 1:3-14)

It is here then, in Christ Jesus, that human freedom
and divine power are brought together for Jesus is both
God and man. In Him, through faith, we achieve the
perfection of our humanity which is in fact a sharing
in the perfection of God. The Holy Bible describes Jesus:

He is the image of the unseen God
and the first born of all creation,
for in him were created
all things in heaven and on earth:
everything visible and everything invisible,
Thrones, Dominations, Sovereignties, Powers—
all things were created through him and for him.
Before anything was created, he existed,
and he holds all things in unity.
Now the Church is his body,
he is its head.
As he is in the Beginning,
he was first to be born from the dead,
so that he should be first in every way;
because God wanted all perfection

to be found in him
and all things to be reconciled through him and
    for him,
everything in heaven and everything on earth,
when he made peace
by his death on the cross. (Col 1:15-20)

The Inspiration of Man

Whereas the perfection of God is absolute love and
total knowledge, man's perfection is very limited. God
sees all reality in one constant vision like a beautiful and
completed tapestry hanging on a wall; we perceive only
the laborious process of weaving the one small strand
of our lives, day by day, while missing the great effect.
As a result, we find our strength flagging and our resolve
weakening. We are free to weave our strand here or
there only because we do not perceive the whole effect.
Yet, the Master Weaver does see all, and His love gently
guides the free designs of men so that they create the
perfect vision He has conceived from all eternity, each
creature contributing inexorably to the whole.

God Chooses Freely

Yet, because of His love, God is not content with the
simple, blind carrying out of His will; a will which in
the final analysis no creature escapes. He has freely
chosen to bring believers to the absolute height of the
experience of love, by revealing to them the design of
His tapestry, the hidden plan of His purpose, the inner
workings of the Divine Mind through Jesus Christ.
St. Peter tells his fellow Christians:

You are a chosen race, a royal priesthood, a consecrated nation, a people set apart to sing the praises

of God who called you out of the darkness into His
wonderful light. Once you were not a people at all
and now you are the People of God; once you were
outside the mercy and now you have been given
mercy. (1 P 2:9, 10)

Scripture calls this special election "God's mercy" in
order to emphasize that it is something to which man
does not have an innate right. We are not dealing with
human equity, but divine majesty, divine generosity. In
the long history of God's dealing with men and women,
His choice, to whatever purpose, is frequently not in
accord with human expectations or desires and certainly
not because of merit. Indeed, those who have been desig-
nated for a special task may not even be aware of God's
designs. To believers, however, a rich passage from Paul's
Letter to the Romans reveals the full import of God's
freedom in assigning to His creatures their places in the
working out of His loving plan for all:

> Even more to the point is what was said to Rebecca
> when she was pregnant by our ancestor Isaac, but
> before her twin children were born and before either
> had done good or evil. In order to stress that God's
> choice is free, since it depends on the one who calls,
> not on human merit, Rebecca was told: the elder
> shall serve the younger, or as scripture says else-
> where: I showed my love for Jacob and my hatred
> for Esau.
> Does it follow that God is unjust? Of course not.
> Take what God said to Moses: I have mercy on
> whom I will, and I show pity to whom I please.
> In other words, the only thing that counts is not what
> human beings want or try to do, but the mercy of
> God. For in scripture he says to Pharaoh: It was for
> this I raised you up, to use you as a means of showing

my power and to make my name known throughout the world. In other words, when God wants to
show mercy he does, and when he wants to harden
someone's heart he does so. (Rm 9:10-18)

Now this last line is a hard saying to understand. We
might immediately jump to the conclusion: so what I
do makes no difference at all! But that would not be true,
as we shall see.

Trapped by Failure

The mercy that God shows to His chosen ones is healing. Probably any one who reads this has an intense
desire to do good, to live a holy life, be pleasing to God
and thereby achieve eternal happiness. Yet, when we
are perfectly honest, how many of us are holy enough
to be confident that God will reward us? Many lives—
even outwardly good lives—are built on a fear that we
really are not doing enough to please God, that we have
not quite come up to His expectations for us. We do try
to be good, but we also are aware of our weakness and
constant failures—I lose my temper when I least expect
to. I find I cannot really give the help to someone in my
family that I should. I am selfish when I would rather
be generous. I have a habit of sin that is unbreakable.
In short, I have turned out to be a disappointment to
myself, my family and God.

If, therefore, eternal happiness is going to depend on
my response to what God has given me—the use of my
talents, my avoidance of sin—then my fears are well-
grounded because my weak will is not really up to being
perfect "as my heavenly Father is perfect," and the effort
to be perfect in the face of repeated failure produces profound spiritual anxiety and depression.

Now, obviously we cannot heal ourselves. Our limitations are not something we can cast off because we want to; a one-legged man cannot decide to grow another leg, a blind man cannot decide to see, a sinner cannot force himself to be saint. Some things are beyond our power, which is why we find ourselves enslaved by failure and inadequacy. Biblically speaking, this limiting power that prevents the full exercise of our goodness, and, therefore, the achievement of happiness is called sin. Of sin, Paul says:

> The Law, (today we might call this "religion"), of course, as we all know, is spiritual; but I am unspiritual; I have been sold as a slave to sin. I cannot understand my own behavior. I fail to carry out the things I want to do, and I find myself doing the very things I hate. When I act against my will, that means I have a self that acknowledges that the Law is good, and so the thing behaving in that way is not my self but sin living in me. The fact is, I know of nothing good living in me—living, that is, in my unspiritual self—for though the will to do good is in me, the performance is not, with the result that instead of doing the good things I want to do, I carry out the sinful things I do not want. When I act against my will, then, it is not my true self doing it, but sin which lives in me.
>
> In fact, this seems to be the rule, that every single time I want to do good, it is something evil that comes to hand. In my inmost self I dearly love God's Law, but I can see that my body follows a different law that battles against the law which my reason dictates. This is what makes me a prisoner of that law of sin which lives inside my body.
>
> What a wretched man I am! Who will rescue me from this body doomed to death? Thanks be to God through Jesus Christ our Lord! (Rm 7:14-24)

Jesus Heals and Gives New Life

Jesus Christ is the Healer, the Rescuer. Jesus lifts us up out of the morass of failure and sin by transforming our attitudes and re-directing our desires by His power. Consequently, we no longer live for this life alone, which leads to death, but in Him, we direct our energies to heavenly goals, which are eternal life.

Though your body may be dead it is because of sin, but if Christ is in you then your spirit is life itself because you have been justified; and if the Spirit of Him who raised Jesus from the dead is living in you. then He who raised Jesus from the dead will give life to your own mortal bodies through His Spirit living in you. (Rm 8:10-11)

When we believe in Jesus, He opens the eyes of our mind and we see all reality in a new light—the light that reveals the purpose of life. (Cf. 2 Cor 4:6). By trusting in Him, we are given new power to act—His power. Faith is trust, an experience that Jesus is acting in me according to His promise so that I literally live His life and love His loves.

Through our Lord Jesus Christ, by faith we are judged righteous and at peace with God, since it is by faith and through Jesus that we have entered this state of grace in which we can boast about looking forward to God's glory. But this is not all we can boast about: we can boast about our sufferings. These sufferings bring patience, as we know, and patience brings perseverance, and perseverance brings hope, and this hope is not deceptive, because the love of God has been poured into our hearts by the Holy Spirit which has been given us. We were still helpless when at His appointed moment Christ died for sinful men.

It is not easy to die even for a good man—though
of course for someone really worthy, a man might be
prepared to die—but what proves that God loves us
is that Christ died for us while we were still sinners.
Having died to make us righteous, is it likely that he
would now fail to save us from God's anger? When
we were reconciled to God by the death of His Son,
we were still enemies; now that we have been
reconciled, surely we may count on being saved by
the life of His Son? Not merely because we have been
reconciled, but because we are filled with joyful
trust in God, through our Lord Jesus Christ, through
whom we have already gained our reconcilation.
(Rm 5:1-11)

Moreover, in talking to His disciples, Jesus did not
limit the trust they put in Him to just the unseen spiritual realities—things that were difficult to verify by the
hard experience of real life. He wanted them to be poor.
He wanted them to trust in Him for all things as a sign
of that inner trust in His ultimate healing.

He said to His disciples, "That is why I am telling
you not to worry about your life and what you are
to eat, nor about your body and how you are to clothe
it. For life means more than food, and the body more
than clothing. Think of the ravens. They do not sow
or reap; they have no storehouses and no barns; yet
God feeds them. And how much more are you worth
than the birds! Can any of you, for all his worrying,
add a single cubit to his span of life? If the smallest
things, therefore, are outside of your control, why
worry about the rest? Think of the flowers; they
never have to spin or weave; yet, I assure you, not
even Solomon in all his regalia was robed like one of
these. Now if that is how God clothes the grass in

the field which is there today and thrown into the
furnace tomorrow, how much more will he look
after you, you men of little faith! But you, you must
not set your hearts on things to eat and things to
drink; nor must you worry. It is the pagans of this
world who set their hearts on all these things. Your
Father well knows you need them. No; set your
hearts on His kingdom. and these other things will
be given you as well.

There is no need to be afraid, little flock, for it has
pleased your Father to give you the kingdom. (Lk
12:22-32)

Our Works are the Fruit of His Life

**Having given us the kingdom, God also gives us
the power to win it.**
This is perhaps the key to the relationship of good works
and faith. When a man is healed of blindness, he can
now do things he could never do before. He can go where
he wants without being led by the hand, he can under-
take new works, evaluate and judge things hidden from
him before. Literally, he is a new man; he is no longer
dependent on others, but independent, able to walk without stumbling because he has the light. So, too, when
we put on the mind of Christ and live by His light, we
acquire new values and judge things in a different way.
After his conversion to Christ, St. Paul saw suffering not
as an evil, but as a way to union with God. Consequently.
he embraced pain, hardship and loss with joy and thanksgiving. He wrote to the Philippians:

I believe nothing can happen that will outweigh
the supreme advantage of knowing Christ Jesus, my
Lord. For him I have accepted the loss of everything.
and I look on everything as so much rubbish if only

I can have Christ and be given a place in him. I am
no longer trying for perfection by my own efforts,
the perfection that comes from the Law, but I want
only the perfection that comes through faith in
Christ, and is from God and based on faith. All I want
is to know Christ and the power of his resurrection
and to share his sufferings by reproducing the pattern
of his death. That is the way I can hope to take my
place in the resurrection of the dead. (Ph 3:8-12)

How different is Paul's attitude of willing surrender
from the stoic endurance of pain and the desperate search
for relief that characterizes a world stumbling about in
the darkness of fear and unbelief.

This light of Christ, however, is not a once-given
light. It is a continuing inflowing of divine light, leading
us every step of the way all the time so that at no point
can we say, "I'll take over now and do it on my own."
That would be to revert to darkness. But healed by the
light, and filled with light, I can do what I never could
do when I was in the darkness. In other words, by filling
me with light, Jesus also fills me with the works of the
light—enables me to do the works of light, because I see
with His eyes and His mind and live His love.

So great is the change that God brings about in us
that Scripture refers to it as new life, or re-birth. It is
life in the Spirit which will never end, and it is a totally
free gift—a complete favor, a grace. The Letter to the
Ephesians stresses this when it says:

And you were dead, through the crimes and the
sins in which you used to live when you were following the way of this world, obeying the ruler who
governs the air, the spirit who is at work in the re-
bellious. We all were among them too in the past,
living sensual lives, ruled entirely by our own physi-

cal desires and our own ideas; so that by nature we were as much under God's anger as the rest of the world. But God loved us with so much love that he was generous with his mercy: when we were dead through our sins, He brought us to life with Christ— it is through grace that you have been saved—and raised us up with him and gave us a place with him in heaven, in Christ Jesus.

This was to show for all ages to come, through his goodness towards us in Christ Jesus, how infinitely rich he is in grace. Because it is by grace that you have been saved, through faith; not by anything of your own, but by a gift from God; not by anything that you have done, so that nobody can claim the credit. We are God's work of art, created in Christ Jesus to live the good life as from the beginning he had meant us to live it. (Ep 2:1-10)

What a mystery! God has made us free, and in accord with the free nature that He has given us, He moves us infallibly to accomplish what He has willed from all eternity. "It is God, for His own loving purpose, who puts both the will and the action into you." (Phil 2:13). Because we are free, He moves us gently but relentlessly to our appointed ends—freely but inevitably!

And for anyone who is in Christ, there is a new creation; the old creation has gone, and now the new one is here. It is all God's work. It was God who reconciled us to himself through Christ and gave us the work of handing on this reconciliation. In other words, God in Christ was reconciling the world to himself, not holding men's faults against them, and he has entrusted to us the news that they are reconciled. So we are ambassadors for Christ; it is as though God were appealing through us, and the

appeal that we make in Christ's name is: be reconciled to God. For our sake God made the sinless one
into sin, so that in him we might become the goodness
of God. (2 Cor 5:17-21)

To become the goodness of God—this is why we were
chosen! This is why the gift of the Spirit has been given
us! This is why we have the power to love! To be like
God!

If our salvation and perseverance in good works depended on the strength of our weak and vacillating will,
we would indeed have good cause to fear the last judgment. If it were up to the quality of my love I would be
dubious about the outcome. If salvation were predicated
on my response to His words, then I am certainly to be
pitied—for failed I have—again and again by broken
promises and forgotten resolutions.

But it is not my weak human and faltering love that
makes the difference. It is God's strong, endless and everlasting love poured forth into my soul by the Holy Spirit
when I believe in Jesus that makes the difference. My
love for my neighbor is the effect of God's love in me—
the sign of His presence and the guarantee of His care
and power in my life. Chosen and transformed, my very
desires directed towards heaven with confidence even
in the midst of suffering, I can look forward to happiness
here and hereafter because already I share God's glory
through my gift of faith. St. John says:

If anyone acknowledges that Jesus is the Son of God,
God lives in him, and he in God.
We ourselves have known and put our faith in
God's love towards ourselves.
God is love
and anyone who lives in love lives in God,
and God lives in him.

appeal that we make in Christ's name is: be reconciled to God. For our sake God made the sinless one into sin, so that in him we might become the goodness of God. (2 Cor 5:17-21)

To become the goodness of God—this is why we were chosen! This is why the gift of the Spirit has been given us! This is why we have the power to love! To be like God!

If our salvation and perseverance in good works depended on the strength of our weak and vacillating will, we would indeed have good cause to fear the last judgment. If it were up to the quality of my love I would be dubious about the outcome. If salvation were predicated on my response to His words, then I am certainly to be pitied—for failed I have—again and again by broken promises and forgotten resolutions.

But it is not my weak human and faltering love that makes the difference. It is God's strong, endless and everlasting love poured forth into my soul by the Holy Spirit when I believe in Jesus that makes the difference. My love for my neighbor is the effect of God's love in me—the sign of His presence and the guarantee of His care and power in my life. Chosen and transformed, my very desires directed towards heaven with confidence even in the midst of suffering, I can look forward to happiness here and hereafter because already I share God's glory through my gift of faith. St. John says:

If anyone acknowledges that Jesus is the Son of God,
God lives in him, and he in God.
We ourselves have known and put our faith in
God's love towards ourselves.
God is love
and anyone who lives in love lives in God,
and God lives in him.

Love will come to its perfection in us
when we can face the day of Judgment without fear;
because even in this world
we have become as he is.
In love there can be no fear,
but fear is driven out by perfect love:
because to fear is to expect punishment,
and anyone who is afraid is still imperfect in love.
We are to love, then,
because he loved us first.
Anyone who says, 'I love God,'
and hates his brother,
is a liar,
since a man who does not love the brother he can see
cannot love God, whom he has never seen.
So this is the commandment that he has given us,
that anyone who loves God must also love his brother.
(Jn 4:15-21)

With this understanding of God's saving initiative in our life, His shaping us through love to be the perfect images of His Son, Jesus, there is always the possibility of self-deception. Because it is mystery, and we are basically simple folk who like to make things as easy as possible for ourselves, there is always the chance that we will simply lie back and say, "Save me," without appreciating that salvation consists in the happiness that comes from the life of faith-filled virtue and the exercise of the gifts of the Spirit.

In other words, in giving us the eternal gift of salvation, God gives us the energy and the desire to perform those works of virtue that bring peace and happiness to ourselves and to others. For only the good person can be the truly happy person—here or hereafter. Consequently, St. Paul in his letter to the Galatians, gives us certain signs by which we can always test to see if we are in fact following the will of God which leads to life and not simply our own weak will which ends in death. He says:

> For you were called to freedom, brethren; only do not use your freedom as an opportunity for the flesh, but through love be servants of one another. For the whole law is fulfilled in one word, "You shall love your neighbor as yourself." But if you bite and devour one another take heed that you are not consumed by one another.
>
> But I say, walk by the Spirit, and do not gratify the desires of the flesh. For the desires of the flesh are against the flesh; for these are opposed to each other, to prevent you from doing what you would. But if you are led by the Spirit you are not under the law. Now the works of the flesh are plain: fornication, impurity, licentiousness, idolatry, sorcery, enmity, strife, jealousy, anger, selfishness, dissension, party spirit, envy, drunkenness, carousing, and the like. I warn you, as I warned you before, that those who do such things shall not inherit the kingdom of God. But the fruit of Spirit is love, joy, peace, patience, kindness, goodness, faithfulness, gentleness, self-control; against such things there is no law. And those who belong to Christ Jesus have crucified the flesh with its passions and desires.
>
> If we live by the Spirit let us walk by the Spirit. Let us have no self-conceit, no provoking of one another, no envy of one another. (Gal 5:13-26—RSV)

How deep is the mystery of predestination we have explored! How convenient it would be to say that we simply merited heaven by our works, or to say that God gives it to us all without any effort on our part. Yet, the truth of the mystery unites the two: God moves us to desire, to act and to achieve. For this reason, Paul writes:

> That will explain why, ever since the day he told us, we have never failed to pray for you, and what we ask God is that through perfect wisdom and spiritual understanding you should reach the fullest knowledge of his will. So you will be able to lead the kind of life which the Lord expects of you, a life acceptable to him in all its aspects; showing the results in all the good actions you do and increasing your knowledge of God. You will have in you the strength, based on his own glorious power, never to give in, but to bear anything joyfully, thanking the Father who has made it possible for you to join the saints and with them to inherit the light.
>
> Because that is what he has done: he has taken us out of the power of darkness and created a place for us in the kingdom of the Son that he loves, and in him, we gain our freedom, the forgiveness of our sins. (Col 1:9-14)

But the question is, "Why?" Why does God's grace seem to bear fruit in some and not in others? Granted He is free to do what He wills and no man can oppose Him, why does He treat different men in different ways? Why are some people beautiful, rich and generous, and others poor, sickly and selfish? Why does he bless and curse?

There is, of course, no clear and easy answer. Paul, after considering the questions deeply in his letter to the Romans, seems finally to throw up his hands in praise at ever fathoming the divine mind when he says:

> How rich are the depths of God—how deep his

wisdom and knowledge—and how impossible to
penetrate his motives or undrstand his methods!
Who could ever know the mind of the Lord? Who
could ever be his counsellor? Who could ever give
him anything or lend him anything? All that exists
comes from him; all is by him and for him. To him
be glory for ever! Amen. (Rm 11:33-36)

Indeed, men have always asked the question why.
When Job thought he was being rejected by God, all his
friends gathered round him and told him he must have
sinned. In fact, even Jesus' own disciples thought all
suffering was caused by sin. When they saw a man who
had been blind from birth, they asked, "Rabbi, who
sinned, this man or his parents, for him to have been
born blind?" Jesus answered. "Neither he nor his parents
sinned; he was born blind so that the works of God might
be displayed in him." (Jn 9:2-3)

Jesus always answered in the same vein. Although
God is sovereignly free to bestow His gifts wherever He
wills, His gifts always reveal His glory, power and love.
Since the greatest of God's gifts is Jesus Christ it follows
that all who believe in Jesus experience the full glory of
God Himself—imperfectly in this life, perfectly in the
next. St. John writes of Jesus:

But to all who did accept him
he gave power to become children of God,
to all who believe in the name of him
who was born not out of human stock
or urge of the flesh
or will of man
but of God himself.
The Word was made flesh,
he lived among us,
and we saw his glory,

the glory that is his as the only Son of the Father, full of grace and truth. (Jn 1:12-14)

Paul, on the other hand, is quite blunt about the limits we creatures have in questioning God about his intentions:

But what right have you, as a human being, to cross-examine God? The pot has not the right to say to the potter: Why did you make me this shape? Surely a potter can do what he likes with the clay? It is surely for him to decide whether he will use a particular lump of clay to make a special pot or an ordinary one?
Or else imagine that although God is ready to show his anger and display his power, yet he patiently puts up with the people who make him angry, however much they deserve to be destroyed. He puts up with them for the sake of those other people, to whom he wants to be merciful, to whom he wants to reveal the richness of his glory, people he had prepared for this glory long ago. Well, we are those people; whether we were Jews or pagans we are the ones he has called. (Rm 9:20-24)

Whatever the abstract, theological problems that are raised by the concept of predestination, the Holy Bible always addresses itself to the question of what God is doing personally for me and what I am doing for others.

The life and death of each of us has its influence on others; if we live, we live for the Lord; and if we die, we die for the Lord, so that alive or dead we belong to the Lord. This explains why Christ both died and came to life, it was so that he might be Lord both of the dead and of the living. (Rm 14:7-9)

The question, therefore, is not impersonal speculation about divine justice or injustice, universal salvation, or the case of the aboriginal savage in a far off land who has never had the opportunity to hear the gospel message. The real question is what I, a believer have done and am doing with my precious gifts of the Spirit given in baptism to aid my neighbor to come to a knowledge of the truth which will make him free. (Cf. Jn 8:32). What have I done to share my experience of faith in Jesus Christ with over 100 million fellow-Americans who have not accepted Jesus Christ as their Lord and Saviour? Jesus Himself tells us in the gospel according to John:

God loved the world so much
that he gave his only Son,
so that everyone who believes in him may not be lost
but may have eternal life.
For God sent his Son into the world
not to condemn the world,
but so that through him the world might be saved.
No one who believes in him will be condemned.
(Jn 3:16-18)

Revelation assures us that no matter how mysterious it seems to our limited minds, God's plan is to bring happiness to all. St. Paul tells Timothy: "He wants everyone to be saved and reach full knowledge of the truth." (Tm 2:4). Yet, His gift of salvation is being offered to evil and contrary men at war with each other and with God. Consequently, the manner of bestowing the gift quite transcends our understanding. However, this gift of salvation begins with the experience itself that God is indeed Love and that His love is always exercised for our good.

We know that by turning everything to their good,

God cooperates with all those who love him, with
all those that he has called according to his purpose.
They are the ones he chose specially long ago and
intended to become true images of his Son so that
his Son might be the eldest of many brothers. He
called those he intended for this; those he called he
justified, and with those he justified he shared his
glory. (Rm 8:28-30)

Conclusion

No one writing can possibly summarize the teaching
of the Sacred Scriptures and the Church or hope to
answer all the questions raised by the mystery we have
been considering. Touching as we have the most secret
intentions of the inexhaustible Divine Mind and the
most profound depths of infinite Divine Love, we can
only trust that as we grow in the Lord, all will be revealed to us in the Spirit. For this reason, in addition
to the usual sacramental life of Catholics, the Church
urges each of us to read the Sacred Scriptures each day:

From the Scriptures you can learn the wisdom
that leads to salvation through faith in Christ Jesus.
All scripture is inspired by God and can profitably
be used for teaching, for refuting error, for guiding
people's lives and teaching them to be holy. This
is how the man who is dedicated to God becomes
fully equipped and ready for any good work.
(2 Tm 3:15-17)

As we search the Scriptures in order to enter more
fully into the mystery of Christ saving us and making
us holy, St. Paul's prayer for his beloved Ephesians remains a prayer for each of us:

Out of his glory, may he give you the power

through his Spirit for your hidden self to grow strong, so that Christ may live in your hearts through faith, and then, planted in love and built on love, you will with all the saints have strength to grasp the breadth and the length, the height and the depth, until, knowing the love of Christ, which is beyond all knowledge, you are filled with the utter fullness of God.

Glory be to him whose power, working in us, can do infinitely more than we can ask or imagine; glory be to him from generation to generation in the Church and in Christ Jesus for ever and ever. Amen. (Ep 3:16-21)

APPENDIX B

PERSONAL SERMON EVALUATION

The following questions are offered to stimulate the preacher's reflection on the content and effectiveness of his own preaching.

1) Are you preaching the gospel message itself, or only the response to the message? Are you giving Good News or good advice?

2) Is your sermon addressed to a need or problem your audience is experiencing in their ordinary lives? Does it answer their unspoken but real question: "So What?"

3) Have you illustrated the depths of the problem imaginatively and realistically?

4) Have you experienced for yourself, in your own life, the vital truth of your biblical mesage, or is it still distant from you—more of an abstract ideal than a living, experienced reality?

5) Does your sermon bring **you** closer to the person of Jesus?

6) Does the language and structure you use reveal your own personal involvement in the gospel message?

7) Have you developed the gospel truths through specific illustrations, stories or examples?

8) Is this sermon a "breakthrough" for you?